Tail-End Charlie

And Other Tales of Aerial Combat over North Vietnam

by

Art Long

1stBooks – rev. 03/14/02

Dedicated to my grandson Eric. May his generation never become involved in another Vietnam.

Photo Credits

All photos were taken by Art Long with the following exceptions: USS Midway under the Golden Gate, Haiphong Shipyard, POL Fireball, and A-6 preparing to launch courtesy of the US Navy; F-4 and A-6 catapult shots, flight deck at night, F-4 over the ramp courtesy of Evan Nau. F-4 in the wires courtesy of Ike Newkerk.

Cover Photo

Lieutenant Commander Jerry Hodge pilots an F-4N Phantom II with his Radar Intercept Officer, Lieutenant Jay Beltz off the author's wing during a combat sortie headed for North Vietnam.

Table of Sea Stories

Prologue

I found no tranquility in the ocean's rhythmic swells. The unrelenting pounding of the waves against the ship's hull only served to deepen my anxiety. With every wave a knot deep within me grew tighter. That knot started growing the day I accepted my fate. But even though I knew I would die very soon, I was not ready to look death in the face just yet.

I roamed aimlessly around the decks never fully aware of anything but the image of me falling out of the sky into the arms of an angry mob, of being captured and tortured for years on end. Nothing I did could erase those mental pictures. They would haunt me until the day I died. And that would be any day now.

The wind rushing down the flight deck stung my eyes and the smell of the boiler's stack gases made it difficult for me to breathe. But the spirit that lived within me knew I was about to begin a new phase of my life. And my life would change, for better or for worse, tomorrow. I said goodbye to the old, comfortable life I knew and prepared myself for what was to come. Looking up at the stars, I said a little prayer. I knew my spirit would never die and that someone up there would be looking after me. Some way, some how I would make it through this ugly little war.

When I returned to my squadron's Ready Room, several junior officers were huddled around Lieutenant Commander Joe Thompson. Joe was the squadron's Operations Officer. But what made him the center of attention that night was his previous combat experience. The young officers, most of them only two years out of college, were there looking for some little secret, some trick that they could use to survive the hostile environment that lay one hundred miles due west of our current position on Yankee Station in the Gulf of Tonkin.

"Hey Kim! Come join us," Lieutenant Junior Grade Jay Beltz bellowed out. "Joe was just about to tell us how lucky we are to be here," he proclaimed as everyone coughed up a nervous little laugh.

"I know you guys are apprehensive about tomorrow," Joe began. "And I know exactly how you feel because I was there once myself. I also know from my own experience that nothing I say here tonight will make you feel any better. They tell me," he continued, "that you are safer flying over North Vietnam than you are driving on a California freeway."

"You've got to be kidding me, Sir," Jay exclaimed.

"I don't really buy it myself, but that's what they told us in the briefing this morning," Joe replied. "But thousands of pilots survived tens of thousands of combat missions over North Vietnam. So it can't be as bad as you think its going to be."

But we all knew that death and captivity were very real probabilities for us. And we were all terrified at the thought of flying in the most heavily defended area in the entire world.

"Right," Jay retorted. "They've probably got so many missiles now they'll be shooting them at us just for the fun of it."

"It's gonna be bad," Lieutenant Commander Denny Yost lamented from his leather chair towards the front of the Ready Room where senior officers usually sat. "I was here in '68 when we lost a whole boat load of pilots to SAM's and AAA. In fact, I heard just the other day that the Navy lost 382 planes over North Vietnam the last time we were here."

I knew Denny was right. The United States had not bombed North Vietnam in almost four years. That was plenty of time for the North Vietnamese to  modernize their defenses with the latest Soviet-made aircraft, Surface-to-Air-Missiles and Anti-Aircraft-Artillery. Now President Nixon was sending American pilots back into North Vietnam. Just the month before in April 1972, he had ordered the USS Constellation to mine Haiphong Harbor. That same month he ordered the USS Midway to deploy five weeks early so she could join the Constellation on Yankee Station in retaliation against North Vietnam for it's Easter offensive against South Vietnam. That was why Jay, Denny, Joe and I were there. It was called Operation Linebacker.

"XO," Denny shouted as the Executive Officer entered the Ready Room. "You were there. Is it going to be as bad as '68?"

"Listen, I know you are all scared," Commander Chuck Kother said as he ambled up to the group in front of the Ready Room. "But if you look at it statistically, the odds of being shot down are less than one percent."

But Chuck was not a statistician. What he failed to understand, we later learned, was that the odds were cumulative! By the time an aviator had flown one hundred missions in North Vietnam's Red River Valley his odds of being shot down were close to twenty percent.

Later that night Jay and I shared our fears and anxieties about flying over North Vietnam. It was Jay who first broached the subject of being captured.

"If I'm shot down, I'll take out as many gooks as I can before being taken prisoner," Jay stated disdainfully. "More than likely," he continued solemnly, "the peasants will be so angry they'll kill me anyway."

"I can accept death if it's my time to go," I told Jay. "That's what they paid us for and we knew the risks when we joined. I can even handle being shot down as long as they rescue me."

But the thought of being captured and tortured like so many of the aviators I had heard about in my survival training was not an option. I told Jay that I had made up my mind that if my plane was shot up and we could not make it back to the safety of the sea, I would ride it into the ground rather than live a life as a prisoner.

I spent the rest of the night fighting off the relentless waves of apprehension that flowed over me while lying in my bunk. In my dreams I imagined being under constant enemy fire the entire time I was over enemy territory. Every second of my nightmarish flight found me evading one missile after another, fighting my way through endless clouds of flak and chasing Soviet built MiG fighters around the sky. I even imagined dancing around snipers with high-powered rifles and dodging flying kitchen sinks launched by gigantic sling shots.

I had a vivid imagination.

Kitchen Sinks

"Everything I had ever learned about air fighting taught me that the man who is aggressive, who pushes a fight, is the pilot who is successful in combat and who has the best opportunity for surviving battle and coming home."

Major Robert S. Johnson, USAAF

Imagine the apprehension an aviator might feel just before his first combat mission into North Vietnam. Then try to put yourself in his shoes as he crossed the beach and experienced his first life and death trial against enemy fire. Thousands of Air Force, Marine and Naval Aviators faced up to that fear during the United State's involvement in aerial warfare against the North Vietnamese. Now it was my turn.

For weeks prior to the USS Midway's arrival on Yankee Station in May 1972, senior officers with previous combat experience over North Vietnam tried to prepare junior officers mentally and emotionally for what lay ahead. While they reminded us that we had all volunteered to put our necks on the line, they would try to relieve our anxiety with personal stories of survival against North Vietnam's missiles and deadly artillery.

Finally the fateful day arrived, my first mission into North Vietnam's 'Iron Triangle'. We would be part of a forty-plane strike assigned to attack the Haiphong Shipyard. Threat maps in Mission Planning indicated that the strike group would be exposed to five Surface-to-Air Missile (SAM) sites and numerous Anti-Aircraft-Artillery (AAA) guns scattered around Haiphong.

Even though the shipyard was only a few miles from the coast there was no safe way into the target, the Mission Planners told us during the briefing. A direct attack from the sea would require a long, dangerous egress over the AAA infested city. It was always better,

they said, to deal with SAM's at 15,000 feet than AAA at 2,000 feet. The best bet would be a roll-in from the northwest so the strike group would be heading out to sea when they released their bombs. They had plotted a 'back door' route that would take us over the coastal islands east of Haiphong, through Hon Gay, then west along a line of karst-ridge mountains. If we stayed low enough, the 3,000-foot mountain range would hide us from search radars. It might even lull the

2

Vietnamese into thinking we were headed toward Hanoi. Then the strike group would pop up over the mountains, roll-in from the northwest, hit the target and continue their egress to the sea.

Then the Weatherman gave us the bad news. Weather over the target would be thick cumulous clouds with intermittent thunderstorms. We would be in and out of clouds along the route and weather could be a factor in identifying targets and other aircraft.

"So fighter jocks," he cautioned, "make sure you have a positive ID before you shoot off your missiles."

Back in our squadron's Ready Room, Joe Thompson, our flight leader, briefed us on our MiG Patrol mission. We would be responsible for protecting the strike group from Soviet-built enemy fighters. Our patrol would be a racetrack-like pattern approximately sixty miles inland between Hanoi's Gia Lam Airfield and Kep Airfield thirty-five miles to the northeast. After briefing us on the technical aspects of the mission, Joe tried to ease our concerns about flying in the Iron Triangle. He said we had probably imagined everything in the world being thrown up at us, including kitchen sinks. But, he assured us, it was really not going to be that bad. As we were leaving for the flight deck he reminded us of the old aviator adage that a combat mission was "two hours of boredom interrupted by two minutes of sheer terror".

Up on the flight deck the sun was shining and a gentle breeze took the edge off the hot May morning. The deck was packed with over forty aircraft parked so close together there were only inches between them; their wing's folded to conserve space. Our F-4 Phantom II jet fighter was parked aft of the ship's superstructure on the fantail.

My pilot, Steve Modlin, and I performed the most methodical pre-flight checklist of our lives. We had enough on our minds without having to worry about the plane malfunctioning.

After starting the engines and testing the electronics gear, I checked in with the Air Boss letting him know the aircraft was up and ready. When it was our turn to launch, yellow-shirted aircraft handlers directed us up the flight deck to the catapult crew. Using hand signals and head nods, the catapult director guided us onto the catapult track. Then they raised giant Jet Blast Deflectors behind us to protect other aircraft from our hot exhaust.

Green-jersey'd catapult crews attached shuttle cables to hooks under the wings. Another 'hold-back' cable was attached to the back of the aircraft to keep us in place until the plane was launched. Final Inspection crews checked our plane over one last time, giving thumbs up as they headed for the catwalks. The Catapult Officer raised his hand signaling Steve to go to full power. Then he signaled for full afterburner. Steve saluted the Catapult Officer with his left hand.

After a quick look around the Catapult Officer bent down and touched the deck with his finger. Seconds later we were being hurled into space at a hundred and fifty miles an hour.

We joined up on Joe and his Radar Intercept Officer Ben Thompson and took on several thousand pounds of fuel from the overhead refueling tanker, then rendezvoused with the strike group. As soon as we checked in with the Strike Leader he headed the forty-plane formation off towards our coast-in point, a group of islands called Ill De Coc Ba. In route the Strike Leader gradually descended to an altitude of 500 feet to keep the Vietnamese from launching missiles at us from nearby Haiphong.

And now it was time for our reality check.

My chest started heaving as I drew in heavy breaths of oxygen crossing the first island. We were over enemy territory. I remember looking around thinking that we were off to a good start because no one was shooting at us yet. Passing the islands we continued north passing over the coastal harbor town of Hon Gay until we were past the eastern end of the karst-ridges. Then the strike group turned west staying just below the top of the mountain range and the dark-blue cloud layer a thousand feet above us. The karst-ridge mountains were beautiful sheer rock cliffs rising from a lush tropical green forest. And no one was firing at us. Four minutes later I heard the Strike Leader call "Batter's up". It was time for the strike group to pop up over the mountains and begin their attack on Haiphong.

We left the strike group and continued on towards Kep airfield. Soon the mountains gave way to a luscious valley. And we still had not seen our first MiG. Our breathing settled down. Maybe it wasn't going to be as bad as I had thought. But we were immediately brought back to reality when Joe decided we needed to draw a little attention to ourselves.

We followed Joe as he turned to the north and descended to 500 feet. Then we circled back to the southwest flying in and out of low hanging clouds. By the time we reached Kep airfield we were traveling faster than the speed of sound. Anyone who didn't know we were there surely knew by now as our sonic booms broke every window on the base. Imagine our gall; challenging enemy fighters to a duel over their own airfield.

As we raced past the airfield we saw dozens of MiG's in revetments but no aircraft on the tarmac or runways. Disappointed that no MiGs were ready to play we pulled up and climbed to 5,000 feet leveling off just above a thick layer of blue-green clouds. But as we approached Hanoi our electronic threat warning indicators began picking up SAM and AAA radar trained on our flight. Was this it? Was my nightmare about to begin? I couldn't get enough oxygen.

My head was on a swivel, constantly scanning the horizon for signs of the enemy. Just as we reached the southern point of our racetrack-like patrol pattern I saw a speck against the light-gray cloud above us. A MiG!

"Bogey, Ten o'clock high, Heading north. Nose up! Climb! Reverse course!" I called as rapidly as I could analyze what I was seeing, giving commands to Steve and our wingman to get four sets of eyes on the bogey.

"Tally Ho," Steve shouted spotting the bogey aircraft high and to his left.

A mile away Joe and Ben were frantically looking for the bogey. But they could not find it. A thick layer of clouds hid the bogey from their view.

"Two, you're engaged! We'll take high cover," Joe commanded, telling us that since we had sight of the bogey, we had the lead and he would take a position above the fight to provide directions if needed.

Steve and I were on our backs as we climbed inverted toward the bogey. I focused on my radar, switching to the 10-mile range, thumbing the elevation wheel that controlled where the radar was looking while adjusting the gain control to get rid of the cloud return. And there he was, a faint green speck thirty degrees above the horizon. Placing the Acquisition bar over the return, I squeezed the lock-up button and told Steve that I had acquired the bogey. I switched to the 5-mile scale.

My radar screen started feeding me critical information about the engagement. It told me that we were four miles behind the bogey, that we had a negative overtake because the bogey was moving north faster than we were climbing, and the bogey was thirty degrees above us.

"Bogey, four miles, 30 degrees up, heading north, opening velocity," I called out over the radio to let everyone know what was going on.

"Buster," I commanded telling Steve we needed more airspeed to catch up to the bogey.

Rolling our fighter upright Steve pushed the stick forward until we were hanging in our shoulder straps in zero G's. We started accelerating. But the bogey was still outside the 3-½ mile maximum launch range for our Sidewinder heat-seeking missiles.

"Three and three quarter miles, 20 degrees up," I transmitted, breathing so fast I was close to hyperventilating.

Another fifteen seconds and we would have our first MiG.

"Sidewinders are hot," Steve called out as he doubled checked his weapons panel to make sure he had a missile pylon station selected.

"One's Tally. Do you have an ID yet?" Joe demanded as he spotted the bogey.

"Negative," Steve replied, his finger on the trigger. "He's in and out of the clouds."

"Three and one half miles. Nose Up, In Range, You've got the Dot," I called turning command over to Steve telling him to look at his radar screen and center the steering dot to get the Sidewinder missile's acquisition tone.

The sound of the heat-seekers guidance tone filled our headsets. It was a loud, growling, buzzing like sound that rose and fell as Steve maneuvered the missile's seeker head to the hottest part of the bogey's exhaust.

Just a few more seconds. I couldn't believe it. Our first mission over the beach and we were going to get a MiG. How many aviators had dreamed of this moment when they were saddled in behind an enemy fighter, ready to blow the aircraft out of the sky and paint a symbolic MiG on the side of their plane?

"No ID yet," Steve barked as he strained his eyes to determine if the rear-end silhouette he was seeing was friend or foe.

"Three and a quarter miles," I called.

We were within the missile's lethal range. Steve was ready to shoot two heat-seeking missiles. We could almost see them leaping from the plane, winding and twisting as their guidance systems commanded the steering fins to ride the heat source to the bogey. But we could not positively tell whether it was a MiG or not.

"He's smoking. Knock it off. Knock it off," Joe yelled as he saw two black plumes of smoke coming from the bogey's exhaust.

Our hearts sank. So close to shooting down a MiG. So close to shooting down another F-4 Phantom!

"It must be an Air Force F-4 coming off a raid to Hanoi," Steve said, disgusted that it wasn't an enemy fighter. The Air Force and Navy never coordinated their strike missions, which is why the positive ID was so important.

We were all stunned. We came so close. We did everything right. All the years of training for this one moment. And some dumb-ass Air Force puke ruined it for us. The only thing that saved him was coming out of afterburner. He had to know air-to-air radar had locked on to him. And he probably figured that only another F-4 pilot would instantly recognize his telltale smoke plume. That decision saved his life and our hides. We would have never forgiven ourselves had we shot a friendly out of the sky over enemy territory.

By now Steve and I were out of oxygen, our four hour bottle of oxygen gone in twenty minutes.

Joe wisely elected to call it quits and led us out along the karst-ridge 'backdoor'. But the Vietnamese had not survived all those years without knowing something about Navy tactics. They were waiting for us and about to give us our second dose of reality.

Passing over Hon Gay a half dozen AAA guns opened up on us from both sides of the harbor's entrance, their tracers criss-crossing our flight path. Steve nosed our F-4 over into a dive for a safer altitude, the gunners' bullets easily following our descent. Steve accelerated and dove for the deck. Now we were down on the water, our powerful twin engine exhausts creating water plumes fifty feet high behind us. Just as we flew out of the gunner's range, another set of guns opened up on Ill de'Coc Ba island, the largest of the karst-ridged islands. Steve jinked back and forth, never staying on one heading long enough to provide the gunners with an easy, predictable target.

Finally we were back over the gulf and the safety of the sea. The living manifestation of my nightmarish dreams of AAA and kitchen sinks was over. And the old aviator axiom turned out to be true once again.

But those were the longest two minutes of my life.

Night in the Barrel

"There are three rules for making a smooth landing:

Unfortunately, no one knows what they are."

- Anonymous

Carrier landings are what separate Naval Aviation from all other forms of flying. The skill and concentration required to bring a forty-thousand pound aircraft aboard a pitching deck makes it one of the most demanding procedures in all of aviation. Landing at night, however, is one of the most frightening experiences a Naval Aviator ever faces.

I remember watching an interview with Neil Armstrong. When asked if landing on the Moon was the scariest thing he had ever done, Neil replied "No, it was landing on an aircraft carrier at night!"

All night carrier landings were scary. But some nights were worse than others. We had an expression for those nights when nothing went right; it was your 'Night in the Barrel'.

One such night occurred while our ship conducted Carrier Qualifications prior to my second cruise to Vietnam. During 'CarQuals' each pilot was required to make ten daytime and six nighttime landings. With close to one hundred pilots waiting their turn, anxiety quickly built up, especially for 'nugget' pilots making their first cruise. To help them, nuggets were paired with experienced aircrews.

As a veteran Radar Intercept Officer with Fighter Squadron-151 with over seventy carrier arrested landings, I was assigned to fly with a nugget pilot we'll call Mack. After several days of watching one flight crew after another qualify, it was finally our turn. We manned our F-4 Phantom II jet fighter parked on the flight deck of the aircraft carrier USS Midway steaming ninety miles off the coast of San Diego, California.

After taxiing up to the starboard catapult the Catapult Officer raised his hand signaling us to go to full power, then into afterburner. Mack pulled the stick back in his lap so the plane would immediately rotate to a nose up attitude. Then he eased the stick forward a couple of inches so we would not over-rotate and end up going straight up. Satisfied that everything was up and running he saluted the Catapult Officer signaling that we were ready to be launched.

The catapult stroke took less than three seconds. In the blink of an eye we had accelerated from zero to one hundred fifty miles per hour. It's the most thrilling ride one could ever imagine. At the end of the cat stroke we made a tight left turn to get into the landing pattern. Upon reaching the 'Abeam' position one and a half-miles from the landing area, Mack began his turn onto the final inbound heading. Lining up behind the ship we settled into 'the groove', an imaginary line rising from the flight deck to the plane. Mack immediately started scanning the vertical glide-slope system called the 'meatball'.

The Optical Carrier Landing System, or 'meatball', sent out parallel beams of light that, from the pilot's perspective, appeared to float up and down. Pilots used the system to determine where they were on the glide-slope. If they were high, the ball appeared above the green reference lights; a low ball seemed to be below the lights. Too low and the ball turned red. Pilots tried to keep the ball centered all the way to touch down.

When I could see the 'meatball' I transmitted "Two-Zero-One, Ball, Five One," meaning we had fifty one hundred pounds of fuel. The Landing Signal Officer (LSO) responded with a "Roger ball".

It was important to make the best possible pass every time, because even on a perfect approach in calm seas there was no margin for error. Imagine trying to land a plane in an area the size of a floating basketball court.

Unlike commercial aircraft where pilots flared the plane and gently touched down, carrier based aircraft flew a controlled crashed called a 'power-on landing'. We literally drove the plane into the flight deck at one hundred sixty miles per hour. The resulting four-G crash provided the best insurance that the arresting hook would catch one of the three wires stretched across the landing area. Just in case the hook didn't catch, pilots immediately went to full power so they would have enough airspeed to safely continue flying.

Just as our main mounts crashed into the deck, our eight-foot long arresting hook caught a wire. A powerful hydraulic system then wrestled our twenty-ton aircraft out of the air by feeding out just enough arresting gear cable to slow the plane down. We came to a complete stop in less than two second. The stop was so abrupt that no one ever forgot to lock his shoulder harness more than once.

Taxiing out of the landing area, we were directed to the port catapult. Sixty seconds later we were rushing down the catapult in what mathematicians call a logarithmic acceleration. Unlike the old hydraulic catapults that smashed its full force into the plane on the launch stroke, the Midway's rotary valved, steam driven catapults allowed a controlled release of energy. So every foot down the catapult you were going faster than the previous foot. By the end of the catapult stroke we were traveling one hundred fifty miles per hour, our twin jet engines leaving a trail of flames twenty feet long.

As we approached the ship on our second pass I suggested that Mack watch his Angle of Attack Indexer. This device told the pilot whether he was fast, slow or on-speed. If he was at the correct speed, the device displayed a circle we called the 'donut'. Otherwise it told him visually to either raise or lower the aircraft's nose to get back to an on-speed condition. I remember Mack being pleased that he held a donut attitude all the way to touch down. Too pleased, it seemed.

We made six more arrested landings that afternoon and finished up the remaining daytime traps the next morning. But as evening approached, all aviators scheduled to fly that night became restless and edgy. Just the thought of landing without visual references caused some pilots to become ill. Nothing sent chills down a Naval Aviator's spine faster than memories of a 'night trap'. And we were scheduled to launch at half past midnight.

16

Finally the hour arrived. It was time for our night traps.

Stepping onto a flight deck on a pitch-black night is a sobering experience that leaves a knot in the middle of your stomach. In that instant you realize that you are no longer in control but are subject to the whims of the sea. As you look around you realize that everything is bathed in shades of red. They tell you it's to hide the ship from prying eyes. But you know it's to keep you from finding a place to land.

Being catapulted into the blackness of night was bad enough. During the catapult stroke, however, the transverse G forces played havoc with your inner ear, which controlled your equilibrium. At the end of the catapult stroke the fluids that were pushed against the back of your semi-circular canals came rushing forward telling your body that you were falling, when in fact you were actually climbing. We were always reminded prior to every night launch to "trust your instruments" and "fight the urge to pull the stick back and climb."

While they hooked up our aircraft to the catapult, we prepared ourselves mentally for the night catapult shot. As a last minute reminder I told Mack not to over-rotate off the catapult. Taking one more look around the cockpit Mack pulled the stick all the way back in his lap and flipped on the external wing lights signaling that we were prepared to launch. A second later we were roaring down the catapult.

Off the catapult we were airborne but not really flying. One glance at the instrument panel told me we were in a nose high attitude. Mack had disregarded my warning and the briefing. So instead of a slightly nose up attitude, we were sixty degrees nose high and about to stall.

"Over Rotation. Nose Down! Nose Down!" I shouted.

Mack immediately pushed the stick forward. The plane banked left as the left wing lost airflow and started to stall. He countered with full right stick and stepped on the right rudder pedal to bring the nose back up. Somehow he managed to get the plane flying again just before it stalled for good. But it had shaken Mack. You could hear it in his voice.

After Mack settled down, I called Midway's Carrier Controlled Approach (CCA). CCA worked us into the traffic pattern. Soon we were abeam the ship at 600 feet. Mack began his left descending turn toward the ship then settled into the groove. I called the ball with five thousand pounds of fuel. At one-eight of a mile the LSO hit his wave off button. Red lights across the top of the meatball began to flash at the same time the LSO transmitted "Foul Deck, Wave Off." The aircraft in front of us was still in the landing area forcing us to go around and try again. Mack started cussing at the pilot for messing up his approach.

On our second pass Mack realized we were high on the glide-slope and too fast. He had to reduce the throttles to lose both airspeed and altitude. Unfortunately he was late bringing the throttles up to stop our descent and we went through the centered ball to a low ball. We had a slightly low ball as our main mounts slammed into the deck.

"Bolter! Bolter! Bolter!" cried the LSO as our tail hook skipped over the number 3 wire.

Had Mack followed standard procedures and pushed the throttles up to one hundred percent when we touched down, pulling the stick back would have rotated the nose into a flying attitude and we would have been airborne again. Instead, we rolled down what was left of the 500-foot runway and dribbled over the end of the angled deck with barely enough speed to fly. By now Mack had pushed the throttles to full afterburner. The 34,000 pounds of thrust generated by our jet engines sent waves of salt-water spray up over the flight deck sixty feet above. I grabbed hold of the ejection handle between my legs. I was ready to eject us if we didn't make it. Mack was fighting the stick, struggling to keep the wings level. After the longest five seconds of my life, Mack managed to 'wing walk' the plane back to flying speed.

Then I heard the most dreaded words in aviation lexicon. Mack said, "I've got vertigo!" Vertigo is term used to describe spatial disorientation. Mack felt like he was upside down.

"No sweat, Mack," I said. "I'll talk you through it."

Since I had no way to control the aircraft from the back seat, I talked Mack through the turns until we settled into the groove with a centered ball. Mack said he felt better and could manage from there. I checked our line-up and glide-slope one more time before looking back into the cockpit to check our fuel. I heard the power come off and looked back out toward the ship. The ball was red.

"Power," I ordered.

"I've got a donut," Mack said confidently.

Our airspeed was dangerously slow, our altitude was slipping under 300 feet and we were still a mile behind the ship.

"Power!" I shouted.

"But I've got a donut," Mack replied, completely forgetting about his glide-slope.

"I don't care what you've got, give me afterburner now or I'm ejecting us," I exclaimed.

Mack immediately pushed up the throttles into the afterburner detent fearing that I would pull the ejection handle and fire both of us out into the blackness of a starless night and perhaps a watery grave. We started climbing back up to the glide-slope. But by now the Wave-Off lights were flashing and the LSO, Air-Boss and even the Captain were screaming over the UHF radio for power.

"Two-Zero-Six, three-quarters of a mile, call the ball," the CCA controller commanded.

Checking the fuel gauge before responding I noted that we had 3100 pounds of fuel, enough for one more pass before hitting the overhead tanker with it's precious cargo.

"Two-Zero-Six, Ball, Three One," I replied.

"Roger ball," replied the LSO.

"Two-Zero-Six, Schoolboy, your signal Bingo," another, deeper voice declared. The Air-Boss had over-ridden the LSO ordering us to execute the emergency Bingo flight profile and land at the nearest airfield.

"Negative Schoolboy, Two-Zero-Six under Bingo fuel, request one last pass," I pleaded.

"Two-Zero-Six, Your signal Bingo. Contact Departure Control on 213.5," was his only reply.

And who could blame them. After scaring the hell out of everyone, no one really trusted us to get aboard in one piece. So we were now at minimum fuel level and had to land immediately. The Bingo flight profile required us to climb to a very high altitude then coast the rest of the way to the airfield. If everything went smoothly we would land with 1200 pounds of fuel. Burning roughly 200 pounds of fuel per minute, that gave us about six minutes of flying time if we could not land at the airfield. After that we were out of gas.

I had been monitoring our range and bearing to several airfields just in case we couldn't make it aboard. I knew that a 90-mile Bingo required 3600 pounds of fuel with a full power climb to 35,000 feet. I instructed Mack to climb to 35,000 feet, heading 088. Unfortunately, we only had 3000 pounds. Our six-minute reserve was now down to three minutes. It was going to be close.

But the worst news was yet to come. When I switched to Departure Control and requested local weather reports, they told us all divert fields were reporting 'WOXOF' (pronounced walks-off) which in aviation parlance meant 'Weather Obscured, Visibility Zero'. The whole world was fogged in.

We were doomed. The 3600 pound requirement assumed a visual approach to the airfield. A bold letter note on the Bingo profile card said to increase the minimum Bingo fuel by 1000 pounds for instrument landings. If we were going to land anywhere along the coast that night it would have to be an instrument approach which required more fuel.

Departure Control apparently reported the weather conditions to the Air-Boss, too. "Two-Zero-Six, Schoolboy request that you Bingo to El Centro, over," the static filled directive commanded.

"Schoolboy, Two-Zero-Six. El Centro is 175 miles. We're 1000 pounds under Bingo minimums for El Centro. We're declaring an emergency. Have Air Traffic Control clear all traffic for North Island," I declared.

Now if my nugget pilot can fly a perfect Bingo profile we might make it.

"North Island, November Foxtrot Two-Zero-Six, emergency bingo for landing, over," I transmitted using our Air-Wing call sign.

"November Foxtrot Two-Zero-Six, North Island. Weather WOXOF, Field is closed, over."

"North Island, Two-Zero-Six, Say winds."

"Two-Zero-Six, North Island, winds calm, dense fog, visibility zero."

As we continued our climb to 35,000 feet, I monitored range, bearing and weather at the three primary divert fields plus the range to El Centro, California. All airfields in the immediate area reported the same conditions and were closed to inbound traffic. We had almost reached our maximum profile altitude when the Master Caution Light illuminated followed by the Low Fuel Warning light. It was time to make a decision. Should we try to land at the nearest closed airfield or attempt to make an impossible idle descent to El Centro? We really had only one choice.

"North Island, Two-Zero-Six. Pray for wind, we're coming in."

"Two-Zero-Six, North Island. Be advised runway is closed."

"Roger, North Island. Copy runway closed. Be advised we either land at North Island or you can send helicopters to search for us when we eject."

"North Island copies. Contact Approach Control on 218.0, over."

"Two-Zero-Six, Roger, switching 218.0," I transmitted as I tuned our radio to Approach Control's frequency.

Upon reaching 35,000 feet Mack brought the throttles back to idle and pushed the nose over to begin our descent into North Island. It suddenly became very quiet. In front of us San Diego lay spread out like diamonds glistening on a black velvet pillow. The huge Coronado Bay Bridge jutting out of the fog pointed directly to the airfield at the western tip of Coronado Island. North Island Naval Air Station was clearly visible. That would not be the case when we slipped under the layer of fog protecting the runway from pilots desperate for a place to land.

"Approach, November Foxtrot Two-Zero-Six, Inbound F-4, Emergency bingo, fuel under 1000 pounds, over."

"November Foxtrot Two-Zero-Six, Approach. Radar contact. Turn right heading 093, descend to 10,000 feet."

Approach Control vectored us directly to the field instead of taking us all the way out to the Initial Approach Point some twenty miles out of our way. He

24

knew we were extremely low on fuel and was trying everything he could to take us on the shortest route possible. A few heading changes later and we were lined up for runway Two Nine.

"Two-Zero-Six, Five miles from runway, check landing gear down."

"Negit, Approach. We'll hold the gear to the last second. We don't have enough fuel to fly gear down."

At three miles we entered the fog. Our landing lights created an illusion of suspended animation as the light reflected off the white haze of the clouds. There were no references, nothing to give us a clue where we were, where the runway was, or if we were even moving. Just dense white clouds. On top of that, our fuel gauge read zero pounds of fuel. Mack put the landing gear down. We were living on borrowed time.

"Two-Zero-Six, Approach. Turn left to final heading two nine zero. Further transmissions need not be acknowledged."

"Two-Zero-Six, On glide-slope. Drifting left, turn right two nine three."

"Two-Zero-Six, Turn left heading two nine zero."

"Two-Zero-Six, One half mile. If field not visible execute published Missed Approach Procedures, contact North Island tower on 231.6," Approach Control recited as if it were just another approach to a fogged in airfield on a starless night.

"Approach, Two-Zero-Six. We're out of fuel, field not in sight, continuing approach. Landing gear is down, over."

"Roger Two-Zero-Six, One Quarter mile. Show you at 125 feet. Do you have the field in sight? Over."

"No Joy, Approach," I replied. We were still in the goo and could not see anything.

"Two-Zero-Six, Over landing threshold."

Our radar altimeter showed us at fifty feet and we were still in the clouds. All we knew was that we were somewhere over the airfield. Then I caught a glimpse of the runway lights off our right wing. Mack immediately banked the plane to the right then back to the left as we crossed the runway. A second later the main landing gear touched down. As the nose wheels made contact with the concrete Mack pulled the Drag Chute handle releasing the Drogue Chute into the wind stream which pulled out the main Drag Chute. With the Drag Chute fully deployed we began to slow down.

Then the unimaginable happened. We flamed out. Halfway down the runway our engines died. Knowing that we would soon be without electrical power I requested a tow truck. Finally the plane came to a stop. We just sat there at the end of the runway in silence. We were safe, shaken but safe. Had we elected any other course of action we would have lost the plane and possibly our lives.

The next morning Mack and I flew back to the ship and completed our six night traps. After that I never flew with him again. I came close a couple of times but always managed to find someone to take my place.

And to this day I still have nightmares about my 'Night in the Barrel'.

World's Greatest Fighter Pilot

"Fight to fly, fly to fight, fight to win"

Motto, U.S. Navy Fighter Weapons School (TOPGUN)

The USS Midway holds the honor of downing the first and the last MiGs of the Vietnam conflict. The first MiG downing came on June 17, 1965 when Commander Thomas Page and Lieutenant Jon Smith shot down a MiG-17 south of Hanoi. The USS Midway's Air-Wing then proceeded to shoot down the next two MiGs of the war. Midway's own Lieutenant Kolvaleski and Lieutenant Wise of VF-161 shot down the last MiG on January 12, 1973.

VF-161 'Rock Rivers' shot down a total of five Soviet built MiGs during Midway's 1972-1973 cruise to North Vietnam. But the Vietnamese took their own revenge by shooting down two of the Rock's F-4 Phantom II jet fighters. Had the enemy known, they would have found a bittersweet satisfaction in knowing that both downed aircraft carried MiG killer aircrews. Of the eight crewmen involved with the Rock's MiG kills, one was shot down and captured and another crewman was rescued after being shot down only two days after getting his MiG.

Within the first week of our arrival on Yankee Station a pair of VF-161 F-4's tangled with two MiGs. The MiGs lost gaining Lieutenant Bartholamy and his Radar Intercept Office Lieutenant Brown and their wingman Lieutenant Arwood and his Radar Intercept Office Lieutenant Bell the first MiGs to adorn Rock River aircraft.

Six days later one of the most colorful fighter pilots to ever don a Nomex flight suit would bag not one, but two MiGs within minutes of each other. Not only was Lieutenant Commander 'Mugs' McKeown a colorful pilot, he was the most egotistical individual I had ever met. I somehow always managed to fly against Mugs when we were in the F-4 Replacement Air Group training squadron at Fighter Town USA, otherwise known as Miramar Naval Air Station in San Diego California. If we made a simulated Sidewinder shot on him in a one-on-one Air Combat Maneuvering (ACM) training sortie, he would claim in the debrief that throughout the dogfight he was behind us and that he had made a perfect shot on us. If he flew against multiple bogies, he would always claim to have shot down every single one of them, no matter what actually happened in the air.

We all felt like puking when he would proclaim during the debrief that he was the 'World's Greatest Fighter Pilot'.

But things would change after Mugs got his MiGs. On May 24th, Mugs and his Radar Intercept Officer (RIO), Jack Ensch, were on MIGCAP patrol just off the coast of Haiphong when Red Crown, the controlling agency for all Navy traffic in and out of North Vietnam, issued a MiG warning over the Guard emergency radio channel.

"Red Crown on Guard. Bandits, Bandits, Bullseye zero three zero at three five miles," the controller called telling everyone tuned into the Guard channel that MiG aircraft were airborne thirty-five miles northeast of Hanoi, which put them right over Kep Airfield. That same controller came up on Mug's frequency and gave him a vector to the MiGs.

"Rock River, we have confirmed bandits at your 278 for 75 miles. You are cleared in hot."

Mugs immediately accelerated his two-plane flight to 600 knots so they could jump the MiGs before they attacked the strike group. He told 'Rookie,' his wingman, to arm his missiles. As the two F-4s closed in on the MiGs, Jack began a methodical radar search for the MiGs. Had they been anywhere inside his radar's search pattern he would have seen them, unless they were down in the weeds where the radar could not penetrate. If Jack had pointed the radar's antenna down towards the ground it would have returned nothing but clutter. Newer models of the F-4 had Doppler radar that could search by velocity, completely ignoring the ground return. So Mugs took the flight down to 500 feet to give Jack a better lookup angle.

Finally Mugs spotted a MiG off his right wing heading in the opposite direction. According to Mugs, "the first move after the tally-ho was a cross turn that put Rookie on the deck with MiGs all over his ass. I went high and suddenly the only difference was that I was at about 2,000 feet with MiGs all over me."

Rookie was fighting the battle of his life. The MiG was right on his tail. He tried every defensive maneuver he knew but the MiG stayed on him. Now he was down in the weeds, tracers from the MiG's twenty-millimeter cannon whizzing past his canopy. He would be dead meat unless Mugs got a shot off in the next few seconds.

Meanwhile, Mugs had saddled in behind the MiG with a good radar lock-on and a solid Sidewinder bogey acquisition tone in his headsets. They launched a heat-seeking missile at two miles and watched it twist and turn as it made course corrections on its deadly intercept.

"Fox Two," Mugs transmitted to let everyone know he had just launched a Sidewinder missile.

After a ten second flight the Sidewinder reached its target and exploded, engulfing the MiG in a ball of flames.

But Mugs did not have time for celebration. A second MiG was closing in on him from his high eight o'clock position. Recalling all of his ACM training, he knew he had to bend the plane back around to his left and break the MiG's tracking solution. So Mugs shoved the stick left then pulled it back as hard as he could. The plane initially rolled left and started to turn back toward the MiG. But before Mugs and Jack could even blink the plane flipped back to the right and they found themselves inverted looking at the tops of tree rushing by their canopies. Their aircraft had departed from normal flight due to the excessive forces Mugs had applied to the control surfaces. Mugs thought he was a goner. It was as close as he had ever come to death. And it scared the hell out of him.

Fortunately for Mugs and Jack, the MiG thought they were goners, too. In fact, the MiG pilot had no idea where the F-4 had gone. The departure was so quick that the MiG pilot lost sight of Mugs' aircraft. That was his last mistake. Mugs rolled the aircraft upright and pulled the nose up. Low and behold the MiG was right in front of him. Mugs centered the MiG in his pipper and fired his second Sidewinder missile. The MiG pilot never knew what hit him.

Mugs could not believe his luck. Two MiGs! The most recent aircrew to achieve that milestone was none other than the Navy's only Vietnam Aces, Randy 'Duke' Cunningham and his RIO Bill 'Willie' Driscoll, who had shot down their third, fourth and fifth MiGs just two weeks earlier.

Back on the Midway everyone was thrilled that we had two more MiGs, but at the same time dreading what Mugs would be like now after downing his MiGs. We pictured him walking down the ship's passageways with his ego-inflated head so big that there was only room for him and no one else.

But that was not the man that returned from the MiG Patrol. The new Mugs was the humblest man you would ever want to meet. Gone was the braggart.

Gone was the conceited, egotistical pilot that never lost a fight. If there ever was such a thing as self-fulfilling prophecies, Mugs had truly talked himself into becoming a great fighter pilot.

And now that he knew how good he was, there was no need to tell anyone else that he was indeed the World's Greatest Fighter Pilot.

Flying Telephone Poles

"There is nothing, absolutely nothing, to describe what goes on inside a pilot's

gut when he sees a Surface to Air Missile get airborne."

Commander Randy "Duke" Cunningham, USN - Vietnam Ace

Every fighter pilot dreamed of shooting down an enemy aircraft, especially another fighter. They lived it, breathed it, and talked about it all of the time. They perfected their dog fighting skills in endless Air Combat Maneuvering training missions. That elusive goal, however, was reserved for those who were in the right place at the right time. The right place was North Vietnam. The right time was August 24, 1972.

After five months at sea flying from the Navy aircraft carrier USS Midway, our sister squadron had already accumulated four MiG kills. We had none. This did not sit well with Joe Thompson, our Operations Officer. So Joe schemed and plotted trying to figure out how to position himself to get the first 'kill' for our squadron. He figured that our best chance would be on a MiG Command Air Patrol (MigCAP) mission.

His plan was to trick the enemy into thinking that one of our two-seat F-4 Phantoms had been hit. With a numerical advantage, the North Vietnamese might send several MiGs up to shoot down the surviving fighter. If they came to play, we would be ready to shoot them out of the air. Since Joe was the flight leader for our two-plane section, we became the bait for his little scheme.

Prior to launch, we contacted Red Crown, the destroyer escort that controlled US aircraft in and out of North Vietnam. We told them what we were up to and to play along with any requests we made for help or assistance. Soon we were airborne and rendezvousing with the forty heavily armed A-6, A-7, and F-4 aircraft that made up what we called an Alpha Strike. Their target was a munitions storage facility in the heavily defended port city of Haiphong. Since our mission was to protect the strike group from MiG attacks we went in ahead of them and positioned ourselves on a racetrack like pattern between Haiphong to the east and Hanoi to the west. Any MiG attack would come from either Hanoi or Kep airfield to the North of our station. That put us right in the middle of the

'Iron Triangle", the most heavily defended area in the entire world.

Whenever you were in the Iron Triangle, you were under constant enemy radar

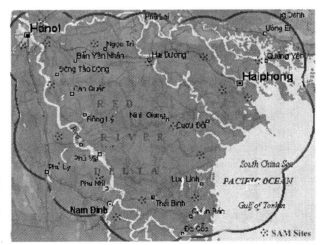

surveillance. To help us analyze the enemy threat, our aircraft was equipped with a raw radar indicator that visually and audibly told us not only the type and strength of the radar signal, but the direction to the ground-controlled radar station. You learned very quickly to differentiate between Surface-to-Air Missile (SAM) signals and the deadly Anti-Aircraft-Artillery (AAA) sites.

So it came as no surprise when Joe screamed over the UHF radio, "Two, we've been hit. Can't hold it. We're going down," shortly after we arrived on our MigCAP station.

Hearing our call, Red Crown transmitted "Switchbox flight, we copy. Launching rescue helicopters. Try to make it Feet Wet". Feet Wet was a Naval Aviation term meaning we were back over the water and out of harms way.

Naval Aviators prided themselves on their ability to maintain radio discipline and only transmit when absolutely necessary. Joe, however, intentionally briefed the flight to chat freely in order to set the trap. Just as I keyed the mike to transmit "You're on fire, Get Out!"; Kaabamm! An explosion rocked our aircraft. I heard nothing but the dull roar of the engines. We had lost all electrical power. My pilot, Steve Modlin, immediately extended the emergency Ram Air Turbine into the wind stream to get power back to our main electrical bus and the motors that ran the plane's hydraulics. I was in the back pushing in circuit breakers, turning off non-essential equipment, and praying that Steve and I would not become the next prisoners of war.

After what seemed an eternity, our radios timed in and we heard Joe yelling "May Day, May Day. Switchbox Two-Zero-Five. We're going down forty miles west of Haiphong." Before I could utter one word over the radio, Kaabamm! Another electrical failure. Ram Air Turbine out, circuit breakers in, essential equipment off and another eternity waiting for our radios to time in. Then we heard Joe say, "Can't make it Feet Wet, Preparing to eject." Great! Here we are, blind as a bat with no air-to-air radar or missiles, no threat warning devices, no electronic-counter-measures equipment, minimal communications capability - and our leader is calling in the Migs!

After several laps between Hanoi and Haiphong we finally got our electronic equipment back up and running. Our ruse, however, did not work. No Migs came out to play. Hearing one Alpha Strike aircraft after another call Feet Wet, we reluctantly gave up our quest for a MiG and set a course that would take us south of Haiphong. Now our thoughts were on surviving the next forty miles until we too could call Feet Wet.

Traveling at over 500 knots airspeed it would take us another five minutes to traverse the rice field covered terrain. With no natural cover to hide us, we were totally exposed to SAM and AAA radar. One SAM site after another tracked our progress. We were okay as long as they just tracked us. But the closer we got to Haiphong, the stronger the tracking signals became. Finally, their radar locked onto our aircraft. The solid, glowing strobe on the raw radar indicator began to pulse. Seconds later a slow, warbling, 'deedall deedall' tone filled our headsets. Our SAM Threat Display Panel lit up a bright steady red. We were at the SAM's maximum effective kill range. And they had just launched a missile at us.

All eyes were out of the cockpit looking toward the threat to catch sight of the thirty-two foot long missile leaving its launch pad seventeen miles away. And there it was, a tiny black speck rising out of a cloud of brown dust and smoke.

As we continued to watch it grow, a second speck began to rise from the same site. Now there were two missiles in the air, both of them headed in our direction. A few seconds later the first missile jettisoned its booster rocket. Now it could receive tracking information and start guiding on our formation.

Inside the cockpit the SAM Threat Display Panel light was now pulsating and the audio alarm in our headsets was sounding a frantic wake up call, telling us we were in imminent danger. As our hearts pounded faster and faster, our senses became acute. And we reacted automatically to years of training.

Our first reaction was to punch out chaff and decoy flares in an effort to foil the enemy's radar. Each plane carried several dozen flares and twice as many bundles of chaff. Each bundle of chaff contained hundreds of small strips of aluminum foil. When ejected from the plane these strips blossomed into a cloud of reflective material that masked the plane's radar image and, hopefully, caused their radar to lock onto the cloud

of chaff. Each time we 'jinked' to a new heading Steve would hit the chaff button and dispense another flare and several bundles of chaff.

Our aircraft was also sending back amplified, and slightly delayed signals in an effort to force the ground controlled radar to recalculate its intercept guidance commands for the missiles. Even the slightest correction would send a missile traveling 1800 miles per hour off course. These counter-measures worked on the first missile. We watched its warhead explode half a mile in front of us. But the second missile was still locked-on to our radar return.

"Switches, let's go down" our Flight Leader commanded.

We rolled over and dove for the deck. Steve pushed the throttles to full power. Hoping to break the radar lock we joined on the lead aircraft and leveled off at 200 feet above the rice paddies. We were literally burning the paint off the leading edge of our aircraft's wings traveling at a speed of 750 knots, almost 850 miles per hour. But the missile kept coming. We tried evasive maneuvers to break the lock. But the missile kept coming and maintained its lock.

The only way to survive a Surface-to-Air Missile attack was to force it go off behind you. And since you could not out-run a missile, you had no choice but to run an intercept on it. Over the years Naval Aviators found that putting the incoming missile just off to their left at the aircraft's ten o'clock position gave them the best intercept angle for playing this very deadly game of chicken. Then at the last possible second, a hard barrel roll around the missile's flight path would force the missile to change its intercept course and explode harmlessly behind you. Or so the theory went.

The obvious risks of such a maneuver was turning too soon or too late. If you turned into the missile a few seconds early the missile adjusted its intercept course and completed its mission. And turning too late just made it easier for the missile to detonate its warhead when its proximity fuse signaled it was close enough to make a kill.

So timing was everything! We use to laugh nervously in the squadron's Ready Room about the old childhood cliché 'One potato, Two potato, Three potato, Pull' whenever someone successfully evaded a SAM. Holding up their right hand while pointing their left index finger to simulate a missile, the pilot would say, "There I was! And when I could read the serial numbers on the missile, I said 'One potato, Two potato, Three potato, Pull'". But they were not joking. The pilot's visual senses told him the missile was close enough and that he should commence his evasive maneuver. But the reality was that the missile was still too far away. So he waited. And waited. And finally, when he could not wait any longer, he still said 'One potato, Two potato, Three potato, Pull'. Then he pulled back on the stick as hard as he could.

So we waited, watching this dark green stick grow larger and larger. Whenever we turned, it turned. And it kept getting larger and larger, closer and closer. Now it started back down towards us in its final few seconds of life. And we were climbing to meet it. Finally the moment arrived. It was now do or die.

The slightest mistake at this point would mean the destruction of one or both of our aircraft and the real possibility that we would either die or be seriously injured and prisoners of war in the Hanoi Hilton.

So, at the last possible second, our flight leader shouted over the radio 'Stand By… One potato, Two potato, Three potato, Pull'. And both aircraft turned into the missile as hard as the pilots could pull. In spite of the 8-½ G-forces on our bodies, all eyes were glued on the missile that was now larger than a telephone pole. And it began to turn. Harder

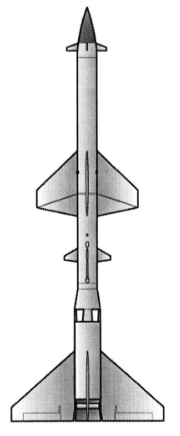

Soviet SA-2 Missile

and harder, matching our turn. Now it was coming right at us. The next second it was exploding off our left wing and under our flight leader's aircraft, engulfing both planes in its fireball. Our planes shook from the concussion as metal fragments from its warhead flew out in all directions. We could practically feel the shrapnel hurling by our canopies.

Flying through the debris we each breathed a sigh of relief and checked each other over for damage. Each of us in his own way realized that we had survived. Not only had we survived, we had beaten death. We fought the SAM and won! That rush of adrenaline brought with it a sense of exhilaration that only those who have come face to face with death can understand.

The image of that moment was indelibly stenciled into my memory. I can still see the instrument panel, the fireball, and almost feel the unbelievable G-forces pulling on my body. To this day I regret not taking a picture of the fireball off our port wing as the missile exploded.

Moments later, Ben Thompson, Joe's Radar Intercept Officer called Red Crown and reported that we were Feet Wet. Now we could head back to the ship and maybe catch a movie in the Ready Room.

"Roger Switchbox, Red Crown copies Feet Wet. Be advised Schoolboy request that you air-refuel and provide ResCAP north of Thanh Hoa. Vector 165 for tanker, over."

"Switchbox copies ResCAP mission. Say squadron call sign, over," Ben requested.

"Its one of yours, Switches," came the reply.

One of our squadron's F-4's had been shot down and it was our job to go back into enemy territory and provide any protection we could for the rescue effort.

Rendezvousing on the A-7 tanker, wc cach took on additional fuel and headed back into North Vietnam. Red Crown vectored us to the location of the downed  aircraft where we circled overhead waiting for the rescue helicopters. But it was too late for any rescue attempt. Our squadron mates had already been captured. Our flight leader called off the helicopters and Red Crown gave us a vector for home.

We made an uneventful landing on the Midway, filled out the paperwork and headed down to the Officer's Mess for dinner. The dining room was deserted since it was already past the normal dinner hour. As Steve and I sat there talking about the mission, an A-6 pilot joined us. So we told him about the how we had outsmarted the first missile and successfully evaded the second.

"So, how did you get away from the third one?" he asked as Steve and I both turned pale.

"I was on a mission to Hanoi", he said, "and followed you out as you egressed the area. While you were evading the two missiles out of Haiphong, they launched a third missile at you from Hai Duong. It detonated on one of your flares".

Steve and I sat there in silence. Moments earlier we had been reveling about defeating two missiles. Now we were humbled when we realized that we had come so close to death, and didn't even know it. It was some relief to find out later that the third missile was the first recorded launch of a SA-2 missile with a heat-seeking guidance system. It was shot ballistically with no radar lockup or guidance. Had it not been for our flares, it would have homed-in on our jet engine's red-hot exhaust.

To this day, when I am driving down the road and absent-mindedly look at a tall brown post, I am immediately back over the skies of North Vietnam reliving those thirty incredible seconds battling flying telephone poles.

Tail-End Charlie

"Airspeed and altitude are like money in the bank...

You can always take some out but can't always put it back in."

Unknown U.S. Fighter Pilot

The USS Midway earned her 'Midway Magic' reputation because Navy Admirals could always count on the Midway to not only complete all of her own missions, but the tasks of other carriers as well. Not only did the Midway pick up additional sorties from the disabled USS Saratoga, she also flew all of her own missions plus those of the USS Enterprise in late October, 1972, earning kudos from Admiral Cooper, Commander Task Force Seventy-Seven.

Throughout her eleven-month cruise, Midway unleashed massive strikes against the enemy day-in and day-out for a record two hundred and five combat days on the line; the longest in the history of the Vietnam conflict. While many of her missions needed only a handful of aircraft, there were certain targets that required Midway's total resources. To insure the complete destruction of these targets, Midway launched practically every available plane against it in one enormous attack. They were called Alpha Strikes.

Alpha Strikes were reminiscent of World War II days when wave after wave of B-17's would strike a target. But unlike World War II bombing tactics where pilots flew straight and level, each Navy strike aircraft in Vietnam rolled-in, one after another from 15,000 feet. The last plane to roll-in had the unenviable role of 'Tail-End Charlie'.

One of Midway's most successful Alpha Strikes was against the Co Chau underground Petroleum, Oil, and Lubricant (POL) storage facility 13 miles south of Hanoi. The route to the target would take us right up the Red River into the heart of the Iron Triangle. Numerous Surface-to-Air Missile sites were located along the way. While on target we would be within the kill radius of some thirty missiles at five sites around Hanoi.

Prior to launch all aircrews involved in the alpha strike attended a briefing to familiarize themselves with the overall plan of attack. While we were busy preparing for the mission, dozens of red-shirted sailors were loading tons of ordinance on the forty A-6 Intruder, A-7 Corsairs and F-4 Phantom II aircraft assigned to the strike. A-6's and A-7's were primarily attack aircraft and had state-of-the-art bombing computers. These computers automatically corrected for dive angle and speed errors. F-4's on the other hand, were primarily air defense aircraft and had no bombing computers. During the attack phase, the F-4's Radar Intercept Officer in the back seat had to calculate the correct drop altitude based on how many degrees they were off the required dive angle and how many knots they were from the planned release airspeed.

In additions to the attack aircraft, mission planners assigned the remaining fighters and attack aircraft to roles designed to protect the strike group from MiG fighters, Surface-to-Air Missiles and Anti-Aircraft-Artillery. Radar domed E-2 Hawkeye aircraft would provide communications and radar coverage during the strike. An A-3 Skywarrior would provide offshore radar jamming.

Fighter pilots loved to fly and fight, but we never really cared too much about hurling ourselves at the ground. But on this mission my pilot, Steve Modlin, and I were assigned as bombers. In fact we were Tail-End Charlie, the last bomber in the last element of the strike group. After a thorough briefing we manned our F-4 Phantom II jet fighter on the flight deck. It was loaded with six

Mark 82, 500 pound bombs. Finally the Air-Boss, sitting in the control tower above the flight deck, gave the signal to launch all aircraft. One aircraft after another taxied up

to the catapults and were slung into space. Because F-4's were notorious gas hogs, Steve and I were the last to launch.

Off the catapult our first priority was to take on additional fuel from an A-6 Tanker. We plugged in and took on enough fuel to top us off. Finally we rendezvoused with the other aircraft circling overhead. When all aircraft had joined up, the Strike Leader headed off for our coast-in point twenty miles southeast of Nam Dinh. We continued flying west another twenty miles inland until we were clear of known SAM sites. Turning to a northerly heading we followed Highway 1A up to the Red River. So far there had been no major threats to the strike group, thanks to the A-3 that was blasting North Vietnamese radar installations with high-powered transmissions designed to overwhelm any radar returns from the strike group. But that would soon change.

Ten miles south of the target our Strike Leader called "Batter's up". That was the signal for everyone to take his final position for roll-in. When we reached the target the Strike Leader transmitted "Let's play ball". Four F-4's assigned the role of 'Flak Suppressors' immediately rolled-in on the target. Their job was to draw enemy fire and take out whichever AAA site was shooting at them. Even if their bombs did not make a direct hit, it would be close enough to keep the gunner's heads down while the strike group delivered their weapons.

As soon as the Flak Suppressors were committed to their bomb runs, a half dozen AAA sites opened fire. The twenty-three, thirty-seven and fifty-seven millimeter guns were spitting fire. Bright tracers leaped from the barrels in steady yellow streams towards the F-4's. These tracers helped the gunners adjust their aim. Those were the ones you could see. For every tracer, there were nine other shells you did not see.

With the AAA sites located, one four-plane bomber element after another pealed off toward the target, the lead plane in each element calling

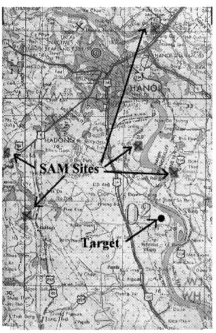

Target Threat Map

"Raven One's In", "Switch Two's In", "Champ One's In"..... Each pilot rolled his aircraft almost inverted while pulling the nose down into a steep forty degree dive. Once they had the target in their bombsight they rolled wings level. Their only job at that moment was to insure their bombs landed on target.

Meanwhile, Steve and I were approaching our roll-in point. Both of us were apprehensive because several AAA sites was still firing their deadly projectiles at the strike group. We figured that by now the gunners had fine-tuned their gunsights for Tail-End Charlie, making us easy pickings. But that was the least of our concerns. Steve spotted a Surface-to-Air Missile streaking towards us. But none of our electronic gear displayed any radar threats. They must have launched it ballistically hoping to break up the strike group and perhaps bring down one of our aircraft. Soon the sky was full of missiles.

We watched the first missile come closer and closer. Finally, when Steve could wait no longer he pitched the nose up and barrel-rolled over the missile. The maneuver used a lot of energy. So Steve nosed the aircraft over until we were hanging in our shoulder straps, floating in zero G's. Steve went into full afterburner and accelerated to get back some of the airspeed we had lost. Now a second missile was coming at us from the northwest. Waiting until the last possible second Steve barrel-rolled over the missile. By now we had lost so much energy we were down to 7,000 feet. We had to get back up to 15,000 just to make our run.

But something caught my eye, a bright flash. I turned towards it just as a huge fireball engulfed the POL facility. I watched the fireball billow up into the sky. And it kept building. Now I was looking up at the mushroom like top of a fireball that was at least 12,000 feet high.

Then Steve hollered that we had another SAM coming in from the north. Nose down; stick forward for zero G's; full afterburner to get the energy we would need to evade a third missile. Fortunately this SAM was not receiving guidance. We broke down and to the right as the missile passed overhead, exploding harmlessly behind us.

Not wanting to venture over downtown Hanoi, we circled around to the west of the target while climbing back up to 15,000 feet and rolled-in on what was left of it. Screaming out of the sky at 400 knots we watched as the fireball's heat ignited one storage area after another. Secondary explosions were going off all over the facility. And one lone gunner was still firing off to our left; his tracer's whizzing past us. Steve dodged them but the determined soldier kept adjusting his aim hoping to avenge the destruction of their valuable petroleum facility.

I put my mind back on the task at hand and began mentally calculating when I would tell Steve to drop the bombs. Coming up on our drop altitude I called out the standard "Standby…", "Mark", "Pull-Out!" commands as we passed through 5,200 feet. Steve pushed the bomb release button and waited until he felt all six bombs separate from the aircraft. Then he pulled the stick back into his lap and pulled it to the right as we began our pullout and turn to a southerly heading. As we were about to bottom out of the dive at 2,500 feet we felt and heard a 'thunk, thunk'. We thought we had been hit but there was no sign of damage.

Our egress took us back along Highway 1A, the same way we came in. We were on our own. We jinked back and forth; never staying on the same heading for more than five seconds least some lucky gunner volleyed a round or two in our flight path.

Nearing Nam Dinh we spied a growing layer of blackish clouds. The Vietnamese were firing their AAA guns straight up in a classic 'Barrage Fire' coverage. So many of the strike aircraft had egress along this route that the Vietnamese figured they would fill the sky with flak and maybe hit something. Steve changed course and went further south. We both breathed a sigh of relief as we crossed the coastline and called in Feet Wet.

The very last aircraft to get anywhere near the target, however, was at that moment taking pictures of the POL facility. This supersonic F-8 Crusader was equipped with high-resolution cameras to record before and after pictures of strike targets. With his F-4 Photo Reconnaissance escort providing cover, he snapped a picture to document our success. That picture showed a mushroom cloud almost 14,000 feet high with thick black smoke still spewing from the inferno.

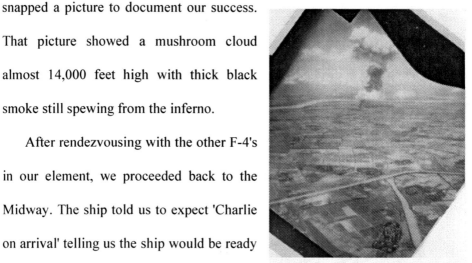

After rendezvousing with the other F-4's in our element, we proceeded back to the Midway. The ship told us to expect 'Charlie on arrival' telling us the ship would be ready to take us aboard as soon as we arrived

POL Fireball Cloud

overhead. When we were within visual range of the ship we dumped the excess fuel out of our fuel tanks. We could not come aboard the ship with more than 5100 pounds of gas.

We made an uneventful landing catching the second arresting gear cable. No sooner had we taxied out of the arresting gear than the Air-Boss shouted, "Two-One-One, Turn off your fuel dumps!"

"Boss, Two-One-One's dumps are off," Steve replied.

"Two-One-One, your spilling gas all over my deck. Now turn off your dumps," was his terse reply.

We shut down the plane and checked out the fuel leak. Gas was pouring out of the six hundred gallon Centerline fuel tank. We counted three holes in it. The strange thing was, one of the holes was on top of the tank.

A few hours later several maintenance Petty Officers showed up with a present for me. It was a twenty-three millimeter armor-piercing projectile they had recovered from the tank. They said that shell must of had my name written all over it because it struck directly below my ejection seat, ricocheted off the keel of the aircraft, then entered the tank where they found it. The other shell pierced the tank a few feet back, ricocheted inside the tank several times before exiting out the bottom. Had the gunner waited a few more seconds until we were out of the dive, his projectiles would have pierced the aircraft and brought him the revenge he so desperately wanted.

I still have that shell. And although I can't read the writing, I'm sure it says 'Lieutenant A. K. Long'.

Smart Bombs

"Any sufficiently advanced technology is indistinguishable from magic."

- Arthur C. Clarke

Long before the nation was taken with Desert Storm videos of sophisticated weapons hitting a window with deadly accuracy, long before Cruise missiles could destroy a target hundreds of miles behind enemy lines, the Navy deployed the first operational laser guided bombs. We did not call them smart bombs back in 1972 because there was nothing smart about them. They simply rode a beam of light until they hit something.

We did have high-tech 'WallEye' rockets that used video contrast to guide it to the target. I escorted an A-7 Corsair on one of the first WallEye attacks against the Than Hoa bridge. Unlike traditional bombing methods where pilots rolled-in from 15,000 feet and released at 5,000 feet, we had to begin our dive from 25,000 feet. We also released the rocket much higher to allow the pilot to keep the target centered in his video monitor until the rocket exploded. It was effective against targets with large, high contrast sections. But it saw limited use due to the lack of suitable targets.

In the early 70's, the Navy began work on a secret weapon that would use newly developed laser technology for its guidance. By the fall of 1972, they had developed a weapon that could deliver bombs with amazing accuracy. Now they needed someone to conduct operational tests under combat conditions. The USS Midway's Air Wing - Five was the obvious choice since we had tallied up more successful strikes against North Vietnam than any other carrier on the line. Considering there were six other carriers on Yankee Station at the time, that said a lot about Midway's 'Can Do' spirit and the seven months we had spent perfecting our bombing skills.

To test this new weapon, the Navy Research Lab needed a two seat aircraft where both the pilot and the navigator could see the target at the same time regardless of the aircraft's attitude. The only aircraft meeting that requirement was the F-4 because of its tandem seated crew composed of a pilot in the front and a Radar Intercept Officer in the back. Although the F-4 was ideal for this project, the delivery method had some serious drawbacks for the unlucky crews selected to illuminate the target.

The Navy chose two aircrews from VF-151 for this project. They spent a week in the Philippine Islands practicing with the super secret weapons. One of the techniques they learned was how to destroy a railroad tunnel. By focusing the laser beam fifty feet from the tunnel's entrance for the first fifteen to twenty seconds of the bomb's flight, they could force the bomb to go off inside the tunnel by refocusing the beam on the tunnel's entrance; the bomb literally flying parallel to the ground as it sought out the laser's return. If performed correctly, the 1000 pound bomb would explode fifty feet inside the tunnel.

But the first laser-guided bomb was anything but smart. In fact, it was all manual and required two aircraft: one aircraft to illuminate the target and another aircraft to deliver the weapon.

Lieutenant Junior Grade Dave Nichols and Lieutenant Junior Grade Ben Thompson, both F-4 Radar Intercept Officers, became the Navy's first combat laser bomb illuminators. They were taught how to focus the laser beam's energy on a target. The most critical part of the illuminator's job, however, was keeping the gyro-stabilized laser beam steady on the target. To do that, they held a black box the size of two cigarette cartons over the canopy rail. Looking through the box, they centered the target in the sight's cross-hairs. They could not afford to let the beam wander because the bomb would seek out whatever the beam illuminated.

You would think that the illuminator aircraft could simply fly in ahead of the bomber and spotlight the target while the second plane rolled in and released the bombs. However, in 1972 lasers were not yet powerful enough to reach a target more than a few miles away. So the illuminator aircraft had to circle the target while the other aircraft's weapons acquired the laser beam. They had to continue circling another ten to fifteen seconds while the weapons aircraft rolled in, established its dive and released its bomb. Then there was another twenty to thirty seconds of illumination for the weapon to guide to the target. It was easy in practice; quite another when Anti-Aircraft-Artillery guns, which were as numerous as water buffalo, were shooting at them.

We tried to look at the equipment when the aircrews arrived back aboard the ship, but it was Top Secret. They could only tell us how they had to deliver the new weapons. I remember feeling so relieved that I had not been chosen for the project. Imagine hanging around a hot target for over a minute circling overhead in a constant, predictable pattern at that. It was insane.

The first test was a designed to take out a relatively easy target in a low threat area so the aircrews could take as much time as needed to deploy the weapon. Their target was a truck park forty miles north of Vinh and about five miles from the coast along Highway 1A. There were no known Surface-to-Air Missiles or AAA sites in the area.

Lieutenant Commander Joe Thompson, Ben Thompson and the delivery pilot briefed behind closed doors. Before manning their aircraft, Ben retrieved the black box from the Intelligence Officer who kept it under lock and key. Meanwhile the new laser guided 1000 pound bombs with their electronically controlled guidance fins were loaded onto the delivery aircraft. The crews manned their aircraft and launched with a dozen other aircraft on separate, unrelated missions.

Since this was the first combat test, the delivery aircraft, an A-7 Corsair, took up a twenty-mile trail behind the illuminator aircraft to give them plenty of time to acquire the target and start illuminating. Ben spotted the target first and called Joe's eyes onto the truck park. It was partially hidden by a thick canopy of trees and palm branches. Ben let the delivery aircraft know they had acquired the target. While Joe established his fixed bank turn around the target, Ben lifted the black box onto the canopy railing. He fired up the laser. An invisible beam shot out of the box. Looking through the sight, Ben positioned the target in the cross-hairs. He had to hold the target centered while the bombs were in flight.

The laser beam hit the cab of a truck and immediately reflected back into space. At the same moment, the detection gear in the delivery aircraft picked up the laser beam. The only thing left to do was for the pilot to identify the target, roll-in, and release his bombs. By the time he was ready to roll in, Joe and Ben were starting their second orbit around the target.

"Two's in," the A-7 pilot transmitted over the radio to alert Joe and Ben that he was rolling in on the target.

The A-7 pilot rolled inverted at 25,000 feet and pulled the nose down into a forty degree dive. Centering the truck park in his bombing gunsight, he rolled wings level and began a seven thousand foot dive. The pilot monitored the bombing computer through his heads up display making sure he stayed within the laser bomb's drop parameters. Passing through 18,000 feet, he pushed the bomb release button.

The bombs acquired the laser beam. Inside the bombs' guidance compartments, a laser light sensor determined if the bomb was riding the beam or drifting off and losing the signal. If the signal was growing weaker, the sensor issued a command to the guidance fins to reestablish it back on the beam. They almost looked like dolphins in flight, constantly moving up and down as they maneuvered to regain the beam. The bombs hit the target destroying a number of trucks and digging craters ten feet deep. The first operational combat test was a success.

The real test, however, came a few days later when Naval Intelligence identified a warehouse outside of Vinh, North Vietnam. They thought it would be a good test of the laser bomb's accuracy because of its proximity to non-military targets. It also had a corrugated metal roof that would help reflect the laser beam back to the delivery aircraft. If this test were successful, it would open a whole new era in pinpoint aerial-bombardment technology.

The city of Vinh sat along a wide, muddy river ten miles from the Gulf of Tonkin. Numerous Anti-Aircraft-Artillery guns and a Surface-to-Air Missile site protected it. This time, Dave Nichols and his pilot, Lieutenant Commander "Hot Dog" Brown, would illuminate the target. Since they wanted the absolute minimum time on target, they elected to approach the target from the northeast.

Hot Dog wanted to make one wide, sweeping, one hundred and twenty degree turn and exit to the east or, if they were still illuminating the target, out to the north. The A-7 would be right behind them ready to roll-in the second it detected the laser beam. At least that was the plan. And as sometimes happened, things did not go according to plan.

Hot Dog approached the target at 12,000 feet heading southwest along the northern outskirts of the city. He purposely slowed to 350 knots to give Dave time to acquire the warehouse. Dave, who had memorized the aerial reconnaissance photos, immediately illuminated the target.

Except for a minor catch, the plan was working flawlessly. The catch was that the Vietnamese were not going to stand idly by when there was a slow moving aircraft circling overhead. Had Hot Dog been able to listen to the activity outside his aircraft he would have heard air-raid sirens going off. He would have also seen dozens of soldiers scurrying to their anti-aircraft guns while the rest of the town took cover in their underground caves and bomb shelters.

A few miles back and two miles above them, the A-7 pilot picked up the reflected beam, rolled the aircraft over on its back and pulled the nose through the horizon until the target was in his pipper. It was then that he saw the mussel flashes from AAA guns scattered around the city. But the majority of the tracers were not directed toward him, but at Hot Dog and Dave who were off to his left.

It was impossible for Hot Dog to miss the anti-aircraft fire. There were tracers coming at him from all directions. It was also impossible for him to maintain his turn without flying right into the ever-narrowing cone of shells. Hot Dog told Dave to try to maintain illumination as he pulled hard into a 4-G turn, but the forces on Dave and the black box were too great and the beam wandered off the target. Realizing the bombs no longer had a beam to travel, the A-7 pilot reluctantly pulled off target without releasing his bombs.

The A-7 joined up on Hot Dog south of Vinh. They discussed their alternate target. In this case, their alternate was whatever target looked good. We called them 'targets of opportunity'. Not twenty miles later Hot Dog spotted a bridge. Dave conveyed the information to the A-7 pilot who immediately prepared for the attack.

"Illuminating," Dave transmitted.

"Two's in," the A-7 pilot radioed as his detection gear lit up.

This time there was no hostile ground fire. Hot Dog and Dave circled the bridge while the A-7 released its bombs. It was a direct hit. The center span of the bridge vanished in a huge cloud of dust and smoke. They watched as the concussion from the 1000 pound bombs created an ever expanding shock wave that knocked over cars and trucks and everything else in its way.

The two illuminator aircrews flew another dozen laser bomb sorties, sometimes with A-7's, other times with A-6 Intruders carrying 2000 pound bombs. Most of the targets were unprotected bridges far from missiles and artillery threats. After numerous meetings with the Navy Research Lab, they concluded that lasers were the wave of the future, but the delivery system had to be improved. Somehow, someway, the illumination and delivery had to be incorporated into the same aircraft because there was too much risk to the flight crew that had to stick their necks out while illuminating the target.

Years later, the A-6 Intruder was modified with a self contained, "hands off", gyro-stabilized laser targeting computer. Now one aircraft could designate a target, drop their bombs, and perform a high-G maneuver while exiting the hostile target.

Now you know how our modern 'smart bombs' evolved. Not because the bombs were intelligent, but because the designers figured out a way to put both black boxes in the same aircraft.

In the Goo

"Ceiling and visibility obscured by darkness."

Chinese Weatherman during WW-II

Typhoons visited the Gulf of Tonkin periodically throughout the year. When they did, naval aviation activity came to a complete standstill. In spite of our all-weather capability, it was hard to strike a target when you couldn't find it. If you did go over the beach, it would be equally impossible to evade enemy Surface-to-Air Missiles and Anti-Aircraft-Artillery when you were in the clouds and could not see the missiles or tracers. So we did the best we could to avoid typhoons and get back to flight operations as soon as possible.

In late June 1972, Typhoon Ora roared into the gulf. Flight Ops were cancelled while the ship altered course to get out of her way. But after two days of sitting around, the Admiral decided it was time to bomb the enemy again. He told the Captain he wanted to launch some aircraft to 'see if the weather was flyable'. So Flight Ops asked for two planes from each squadron to see if they could see anything, even a break in the clouds that would let us drop some bombs. The directive came down to our squadron. Finding no volunteers, Joe

Thompson, our Operations Officer decided that our section would fulfill the Admirals orders. Our mission was to check out Haiphong Harbor.

After our briefing Joe, Ben Thompson, his Radar Intercept Officer, Steve Modin, my pilot and I stepped out on the flight deck. A heavy mist immediately covered us from clouds that completely engulfed the ship. We could not see the ocean. We could not see the bow of the ship. We could barely make out the silhouettes of our gray aircraft against the typhoon's gray-green clouds. And we're thinking this is nuts. No one in his right mind would fly in this weather. But the Admiral had given the order.

The flight deck crews were shaking their heads. While helping us strap into our ejection seats, our Plane Captain asked me "Are you guys really going to fly in this, Sir?"

"Yeah, we're suppose to be looking for a hole in the clouds," I replied.

I could feel the ship rolling from side to side as we taxied up to the catapult. The catapult ride would be easy compared to landing, assuming we could even find the ship again. They positioned Joe's aircraft on the port catapult and our plane on the starboard catapult so we could join up on him as soon as we launched. A few seconds later we roared down the catapult into a surreal whiteness. Soon we were tucked in under Joe's right wing. We dared not lose sight of him because we would never find him again in this weather.

We reported back to Midway periodically that we were 'Popeye' as we climbed to 30,000 feet then on to 40,000 feet. There were no tops to the clouds. It got brighter and brighter the higher we went. But we were still in the clouds. We flew close to the coastline. There was nothing to see, only white clouds.

All ten aircraft on the launch reported the same weather conditions from all over the operating area. The entire gulf was inundated with clouds. Seeing no purpose in keeping us flying in the goo, Midway ordered us back for recovery. They gave each aircraft specific instructions on where and when to commence his approach.

We circled around the carrier's holding pattern for another half an hour while the ship prepared to recover aircraft. Because of the limited flight deck space, each launch/recovery cycle required planes to be moved from one end of the ship to the other. Prior to launch, all aircraft were moved from the ship's bow to the landing area and one of three aircraft elevators. These elevators were so large they could lift two jet fighters at once. As each plane scheduled for launch taxied up to the catapult, it effectively cleared the landing area for the recovery that would commence immediately after the last aircraft launched. Those aircraft that were still in the landing area were moved to the bow. As each aircraft landed the pilot would taxi up the bow and park as close as possible to the other aircraft. This cycle was played out every hour and a half, twelve hours a day, every day for thirty to forty-five days while we were at sea.

Finally it was our turn to commence our approach. Still in the goo, we proceeded down to 250 feet and three-quarters of a mile behind the ship. We should have seen the ship by now. Finally the dark gray image of the ship appeared, but at something less than a quarter of a mile. Four seconds later we planted the main-mounts down on the deck catching the number two wire. It was the first time we had seen anything but white since being catapulted off the front end two hours earlier.

We reported to the Admiral that the weather was not flyable.

AAA Gunnery School

"Nothing makes a man more aware of his capabilities and of his limitations than

those moments when he must push aside all the familiar defenses of ego and

vanity, and accept reality by staring, with the fear that is normal to a man in

combat, into the face of Death."

Major Robert S. Johnson, USAAF

27 Victories, WW-II

During the USS Midway's eleven-month cruise to Vietnam in 1972, we lost

close to two dozen pilots and Naval Flight Officers to Anti-Aircraft-Artillery and

Surface-to-Air Missiles. Yet, as hard as it may seem, flying combat missions day

after day, month after month becomes routine, like just another day at the office.

It was easy to become complacent. After seven months at sea, most of us

thought we had a handle on carrier operations. It began to show in our boarding

rates and the mental mistakes that we made. I remember coming back from my

second Alpha Strike of the day and reading a note on the Ready Room's black

board that they needed a RIO for the last Alpha Strike. I immediately volunteered

for the mission. My logic was that if I could make it through an attack on

Haiphong and another attack on Nam Dinh, I could surely make it through a strike in downtown Hanoi. The Squadron Duty Officer immediately called the Flight Surgeon who promptly grounded me for Combat Fatigue.

Mistakes often brought you to the brink of disaster. One morning we were scheduled for a Weather Reconnaissance mission to see if the weather was good enough to launch strike aircraft. We were catapulted into the blackness an hour before sunrise during a Southeast Asia typhoon. Our two-plane section headed toward the coast. We were in and out of heavy clouds, spending most of the time scanning our instruments. We proceeded to a point just off the coast of Haiphong. At least that is what our Tactical Navigation system was telling us. As it turned out, we were several miles inland directly over Haiphong. Suddenly our Threat Warning systems went berserk. A Surface-to-Air Missile Fan Song radar site had locked onto us. We could hear AAA radar chirping in our headsets as it sought out our radar return. And we were in the goo.

Joe Thompson, our flight leader, immediately took us down below the cloud cover so we could at least have a chance of defending ourselves. We broke out over Haiphong Harbor at 1500 feet. All the ships were still lit up in the pre-dawn hours, their lights reflecting off the low hanging clouds. The rest of the sleeping city was as black as the ocean water below us. But not for long. The Vietnamese communication system must have awakened the entire port because almost every ship in the harbor started shooting at us. AAA batteries close to the Haiphong Shipyard joined in the fray. It would have been a great fireworks display had we not been the object of their contempt. But somehow we managed to get back to the safety of the sea before anything drastic happened.

But what could have turned out to be a deadly mistake occurred when my pilot and I were scheduled to fly with someone other than our regular wingman. Our mission was to take out a bridge southeast of Vinh in central North Vietnam. Since my pilot, Steve Modlin was a junior officer, the lead went to Lieutenant Bruce 'Brontosaurus' Hayward and his Radar Intercept Officer, Lieutenant Junior Grade Ed 'Fast Eddie' Kosky. Ed briefed the en-route navigation portion of the flight. His plan called for us to coast-in just northeast of Vinh then follow the river until we found the Highway 1A bridge. Ed even drew a picture of what Vinh's inland waterways would look like in our radar's terrain mapping mode.

We suited up, manned our aircraft, and launched along with two dozen aircraft scheduled for that launch cycle. One of those aircraft was a KA-6D Intruder. Unlike its A-6 bomber counterpart, it was specifically designed as an in-

flight refueling tanker with four external wing tanks and an external centerline tank. One of the tanks housed a retractable hose that

allowed fuel to flow from the tanker to whichever aircraft needed fuel.

In-flight refueling was not easy. It was not like driving to the nearest service station and plugging a hose into your fuel tank. It took considerable aircrew coordination since the pilot could not look at the refueling drogue as he attempted to push the refueling probe into the basket. If the pilot looked, he would end up chasing the basket around the sky. For F-4 Phantom crews that meant the Radar Intercept Officer (RIO) had to talk the pilot into the basket. Approaching the tanker, the pilot would extend the in-flight refueling probe, then position his aircraft approximately ten feet behind and 3 feet to the left of the tanker's extended hose. The pilot would then add just enough throttle to begin closing the gap between the two aircraft. The RIO gave directions using simple Up, Down, Left and Right commands until the probe entered the basket. Once in the basket, the pilot would fly in perfect formation with the tanker until receiving his allotment of gas.

After refueling, we rendezvoused on our flight leader as he turned to a heading of two five zero degrees for our coast-in point. But something did not feel right. We should have been heading almost due west. I turned on radar mapping to determine our bearing to Vinh.

After comparing the radar's ground return picture with my navigation map, I told Steve that we were not heading toward Vinh. Vinh was off to the right about thirty degrees. Although the radar returns were similar, it appeared that we were heading towards a coastal inlet thirty miles south of Vinh.

"Switch One, Switch Two, over," I transmitted over our UHF radio using our squadron's call sign.

"Go ahead, Two."

"Recommend we come right to two eight zero, over," I said requesting a course change to two eight zero degrees.

"Negative Two, we're okay on this heading."

I was perplexed. Why could Ed be off course so badly? I examined my radar return again. Sure enough, we were south of our coast-in, heading directly toward Ha Tin. Ed had apparently confused Ha Tin's similar looking radar picture for that of Vinh's. And his mistake would come close to getting all of us killed.

"Switch One, Switch Two, over," I transmitted again.

"Go ahead, Two."

"I strongly recommend we come right to two eight five, over."

"Negative Two, we're okay on this heading," was Ed's terse reply. He also sounded exasperated.

Steve and I knew what we were getting into. Ha Tin was the official AAA Gunnery School of North Vietnam. Everyone and his brother trained in Ha Tin. They had more guns there than any one ever believed. And I hated AAA even more than Surface-to-Air Missiles. AAA had already accounted for seventy-five percent of all aircraft losses on that cruise and I wanted to stay as far away from them as possible. Unfortunately, Bruce and Ed had no idea what lay ahead of them.

Finally we went Feet Dry over enemy territory. We continued inland but found no bridge. Then Bruce turned south. Meanwhile I was scanning the horizon in all directions looking for any indication of enemy fire. I really felt uncomfortable. My head was on a swivel looking for that black cloud that seemed to be hanging over my head.

"Switch One, Switch Two, over," I called.

"Go ahead, Two."

"I show us thirty miles south of Vinh, over," I warned.

"Something must be wrong, we don't see the bridge anywhere," Ed replied.

"Two, I've got a bridge in that town up ahead. Let's roll in on it," Brontosaurus transmitted.

"One, that's Ha Tin. We're going to take another target. Recommend you select another target, too," Steve urged.

"Nah, we'll be okay," Brontosaurus said confidently.

"Be careful," I cautioned.

Bruce moved out ahead of us as he swung around to the south of Ha Tin. We watched him roll-in and establish his forty degree dive. Then the whole world opened up on him. They were taking more AAA fire than I had ever seen. It was unbelievable how many glowing tracers were snaking towards their plane. Bruce was twisting and turning the aircraft as he dodged the streams of bullets. Suddenly flames shot out the back of his aircraft.

"Oh my God." I yelled. "They've been hit."

A few seconds later Steve chuckled, "No, Bruce just went into afterburner. They're getting the hell out of there."

We watched as Bruce dropped his bombs way above his planned release altitude. The bombs missed the town landing in some rice paddies a mile north of the bridge.

But I still felt uncomfortable. So I picked up my scanning. I looked off to the right, then to the left, then leaning as far forward as I could, I twisted around to look directly behind us. What I saw scared the hell out of me. We were taking 85-millimeter AAA fire from the peninsula off to our left. I could see a half dozen flak clouds behind us, the well-trained gunner slowly but surely walking his deadly projectiles with their explosive charges up our tail.

"Break Port! Break Port!" I screamed.

Steve immediately rolled the aircraft to the left and pulled the stick back in his lap. Looking back over our shoulders we watched the four-inch shell explode where we would have been had I not looked behind us.

"God, that was close," Steve exhaled.

"Let's get those suckers," I said.

So we rolled inverted and pulled the nose down into a forty degree dive. The gunners wisely chose to take cover when they realized the tables had been turned and they were now the target. We rolled wings level. Steve continued to make minor adjustments in our dive to get the AAA gun centered in his gunsight. At 5000 feet I gave Steve the standard bomb release commands. He pushed the 'pickle' button releasing our 3000-pound payload.

As each 500 pound bomb was ejected from the bomb rack, a copper wire with one end attached to the bomb rack and the other end threaded through the fuse, was pulled free from the bomb allowing the fuse's mini-propeller to start rotating. The propeller acted as a timer. After three or four seconds of flight, the fuse armed the bomb and allowed it to detonate on impact.

While we were pulling off the target, Bruce and Ed were approaching the target from the west at 5000 feet. They watched our six bombs hit the target. Their post strike assessment was that we had made a direct hit. But we did not stick around any longer than necessary. It was satisfaction enough knowing that we had once again survived a most certain death sentence and wiped out a large

Anti-Aircraft-Artillery gun in the process.

Dangerous Real Estate

"Flying is not dangerous, crashing is!"

- Anonymous

Anyone who has been on a flight deck during flight operations knows that the four-acre deck sitting atop the aircraft carrier is dangerous. In spite of all of the safety procedures instituted over the eighty years carriers have been launching and recovering aircraft, accidents happened. And USS Midway's deployment to North Vietnam in 1972 was no exception.

Whenever the Midway was at sea, hundreds of flight deck personnel could be found between launch/recover cycles either preparing aircraft for launch or re-  positioning them for the next cycle. The environment demanded their total attention. Safety was always the top priority.

The pace quickened every hour and a half during Flight Ops as dozens of aircraft launched from the catapults. As the last aircraft was slung into space, the

first aircraft from the previous launch was ready to land. It was during this thirty-minute evolution that most accidents occur. The slightest lapse of concentration could be deadly. Jet blasts sent many a sailor over the side of the sixty-foot high flight deck. Some sailors have been sucked into air intakes. Men whose job it was to free the arresting gear cable from the aircraft's tail-hook have been killed when the cable snapped and whip-lashed across the deck under thousands of pounds of pressure.

Launch and recovery also posed a danger to aircrews. The greatest risk during a catapult launch was getting a 'cold cat'. Midway's catapult ride was fairly smooth, accelerating us all the way to the end of the catapult stroke. But if anything went wrong, we had less than a second to react and pull the ejection handle. Out of the tens of thousands of catapult shots on that cruise we only lost one aircraft to a cold catapult. An A-7 was on the starboard catapult loaded down with six thousand pounds of bombs. When the Catapult Officer gave the signal to launch, instead of pushing the aircraft to one hundred fifty miles an hour, either

the catapult lost power and hurled the aircraft off with insufficient airspeed or the aircraft's engine failed. The A-7 pilot realized his plane was not going to have the needed airspeed. He must have made some sort of effort to recover the ill fated aircraft because we never saw him eject.

The USS Midway also suffered several landing accidents. Equally important to being on glide-slope was being properly lined up so your aircraft landed on the centerline of the landing area. Some large winged aircraft had absolutely no off-center tolerance. On January 8, 1973 Robby 612, an A-3 Skywarrior made a normal approach to the ship. The Landing Signal Officer told the pilot to come

right for line-up. Just before passing over the ramp, the pilot induced a little too much right drift. His right wing wiped out three H-3 'Big Mother' helicopters and nipped an F-4 sitting behind the superstructure. Fortunately, no one was hurt.

The worst flight deck accident of the cruise happen late one night when an A-6 Intruder lost its right landing gear main-mount on touchdown. It could not have happened at a more vulnerable time in the launch /recover cycle. We were in the process of recovering the last launch of the night. Twenty aircraft were parked on the bow of the ship. As each aircraft recovered, the pilot taxied out of the landing area and up the bow to the next available spot. Flight deck crews were busy securing aircraft with tie-downs. Plane Captains were pushing safety pins into ejection seats and missile launchers. Flight crews were debriefing squadron Troubleshooters on problems they had encountered during the flight. There were over seventy sailors and aviators on the bow of the ship at the time of the accident.

One deck below, a number of officers and I were waiting in VF-151's Ready Room for the nightly movie that would begin right after flight operations. Most of us were watching the landings on the Pilot Landing Aid Television monitor called the PLAT. The PLAT's camera was mounted in the centerline of the landing area. Crosshairs identified glide-slope and line-up. We could also hear the voice transmissions between the pilot and the Landing Signal Officer. Every landing was recorded and could be played back if necessary to debrief a pilot. We all watched every approach whenever we were near the PLAT.

One half mile behind the ship an A-6 pilot was making a normal approach to the ship. His aircraft stayed right in the PLAT's crosshairs all the way to touchdown. We watched as the aircraft's main-mounts slammed into the deck and the arresting hook caught the number two wire. Just as the plane started to decelerate, the right landing gear sheared off. The off-balance aircraft's right wing tip hit the flight deck causing the tail-hook to slip off of the arresting cable. But instead of continuing up the angle deck, the plane veered right, heading straight toward the bow.

Our Ready Room was located just behind and below the catapults. We all looked up at the PLAT when we heard the A-6's tail-hook grinding across the flight deck above our heads. This was not normal and only spelled disaster for anyone on the bow of the ship.

"All Hands, Fire on the Flight Deck. Away the Flying Squad," the ship's boatswain announced over the ships public address system.

The ship's emergency crews had been set into action. Fire fighters stationed on the flight deck were instantly on the scene with fire hoses spraying down the burning aircraft. Emergency medical personnel started attending to the injured. All able-bodied men on the flight deck were carrying the wounded out of the conflagration or manning fire hoses.

The quick action of these men prevented a potential disaster that could have killed dozens of sailors and disabled the Midway. As it was, Midway lost four sailors that night. Dozens of sailors, officers and aviators were wounded. The A-6's Bombardier/Navigator, Lieutenant Bixel, apparently ejected. His body was never found. The Commander of Air-Wing Five was critically injured as he deplaned, almost losing a leg. In all a total of fifteen aircraft were destroyed or damaged.

There are countless other stories of brave men whose lives were cut short aboard aircraft carriers. But to those that survived a tour of duty on 'the roof', the flight deck will always be the most dangerous piece of real estate on earth.

Pit Stop

"Every F-4 takes off with two in flight emergencies:

- *It's on fire*

- *It's low on fuel.*

- Anonymous Navy F-4 Pilot

An Aircraft Carrier is always at risk of being attacked. Destroyers, submarines and aircraft constantly surround and protect her. When she is not launching and recovering aircraft, aircrews are strapped into the cockpit of 'Alert Five' jet fighters hooked up to the catapult and ready to launch in five minutes. During Flight Ops she is protected from the enemy by jet fighters flying Barrier Patrols. Positioned between the carrier and the threat these patrols provide a buffer against attacks, their aircrews constantly scanning the skies and monitoring their radar for enemy aircraft.

Barrier Patrols, or BarCaps in fighter lingo, had another name, however, that more accurately reflected the true nature of the mission. We called them BoreCaps. You can't imagine a more boring mission. For an hour and a half you did nothing but fly a racetrack like pattern round and round and round doing nothing more than drilling holes in the sky. And heavens forbid that your relief aircraft failed to launch. Then you were stuck, strapped into the same hard ejection seat for almost four hours.

If you were lucky, you brought enough reading material to last the duration of the flight. Or if you were homesick, you wrote letters. But it was boring, boring, boring.

At least most of the time. Then there were nights when things went to hell in a hand basket and you felt fortunate to make it back to the ship in one piece. Such was the night of December 9, 1972. For three days Typhoon Theresa hammered away at the Gulf of Tonkin causing heavy seas and gale-force winds. When she first arrived the sea swells were so bad that an A-7 aircraft and a tow tractor broke loose from their tie-down chains and slid into a helicopter when the ship rolled hard to port. Later in the week the weather would become so bad they would cancel our midnight to noon flight operations altogether.

In spite of the weather the USS Midway and Air-Wing Five were still flying attack and BarCap sorties. And tonight it was our turn to fly another boring BarCap. After eight months at sea, Steve Modlin, my pilot, and I could recite the BarCap briefing by heart, even if it was almost midnight and the first launch of the night. So Joe Thompson, our flight leader briefed emergency procedures instead, especially low fuel procedures around the ship. As usual, Air-Wing tankers would be overhead in case of emergencies. He emphasized, however, that without a divert airfield, we had to land back aboard the ship. There were no other options. We called it Blue Water Ops.

Up on the flight deck Typhoon Theresa was pounding away, pelting ship personnel with stinging droplets of rain. Drenched to the teeth, we manned our fighter and miraculously  launched on schedule. We delayed our usual in-flight refueling pit stop so the BarCap aircraft we were relieving from the USS Enterprise could make their recovery time. Fifteen minutes later we checked in with Red Crown, the controlling agency in the Gulf of Tonkin just as we had done innumerable times before. We did our cursory radar sweeps to make sure no one was about to attack the ship, then tried to keep ourselves awake for the next hour and a half until our tanker arrived. Since we were between cloud layers I would periodically paint the coast with my radar just to assure myself that we were still on station. Without any visual references, we had to depend on our radar and navigation instruments to tell us where we were relative to some ship in the middle of the Gulf of Tonkin.

Towards the end of our hour and a half BarCap, Red Crown called to tell us the good new and the bad news.

"Switchbox Two-Zero-Five, Red Crown. Schoolboy advises that both relief aircraft are down and cannot launch. The good news is your tanker is on the way. Vector one seven zero for Robby Six-One-Three," the controller told us sounding half-asleep, too.

Normally we would have each topped off our tanks, but Robby Six-One-Three, an A-3 Skywarrior aircraft, was 4000 pounds short on fuel. We would simply have to wait until our relief tanker showed up to get the extra gas. Resuming our patrol we drilled holes in the sky for another hour and a half, the pain in our seats growing by the minute. But the longer we drilled, the less the clouds seemed willing to cooperate. By the end of our second BarCap patrol it was completely weathered in. We were in the goo. Finally Red Crown advised us that our reliefs were on the way and we could head back to the ship.

"Red Crown, Two-Zero-Five. Are there any tankers for us?" Ben Thompson, Joe's Radar Intercept Officer asked.

"That's a negative Two-Zero-Five," Red Crown replied.

We were already at 3500 pounds of fuel. By the time we commenced our approach we would be at 2500 pounds. If we did not get aboard on the first pass, we would have to find a tanker immediately and take on more fuel. Considering how much fuel our F-4 burned each minute, we would have less than eight minutes to find a tanker and get fuel into our fuselage tanks before we completely ran out of gas. And this was certainly no time to be lollygaging around the carrier in a high performance gas hog that was so fast it could fly from San Diego to Los Angles in less than nine minutes but be out of fuel before it got there.

Unfortunately everyone else in the world was low on fuel, too. On top of that, of the three tankers scheduled on this launch/recovery cycle, only two were able to launch. That meant there was too little fuel for too many hungry aircraft. The Air-Boss would earn his pay tonight. Ben called Approach Control to get our landing instructions.

"Roger, Switch Two-Zero-Five, Marshall zero four zero at three five miles. Depart Marshall at zero three five eight. Report Leaving," Approach Control told us.

The carrier's holding pattern was called Marshall. Carrier Controlled Approach (CCA) stacked aircraft at one-mile intervals, a thousand feet apart. The lowest holding pattern was twenty miles behind the ship at an altitude of 5,000 feet. Schoolboy's Marshall instructions told our flight leader to hold thirty-five miles northeast of the ship at an altitude of 20,000 feet. They were to be at that point in the sky precisely at 3:58 AM on a heading of 220 ready to begin their descent. Our holding pattern would be one mile further out and 1,000 feet above them. We would depart Marshall at 3:59 AM. Once recovery began there would be a constant stream of aircraft landing every sixty seconds. And there were fifteen aircraft ahead of us, all on the same radio frequency. We would be one of the last aircraft to land.

We listened as one aircraft after another attempted to land on the pitching deck. Aircraft that had failed to catch the arresting gear were requesting additional fuel. Other aircraft were asking the tanker for his position so they could rendezvous on him. It sounded like a real zoo. And we were about to join the other monkeys clamoring for fuel.

At precisely 3:59AM I radioed "Schoolboy, Switch Two-One-One, Departing Marshall."

We commenced our approach. Still in the goo, we proceeded down to 500 feet where we finally broke out of the clouds. Thank goodness we would be able to see the ship. We listened as Joe and Ben, a minute ahead of us, made it safely aboard. With our landing gear and flaps down we prepared to land.

Moments later CCA transmitted "Switch Two-One-One, three-quarters of a mile, call the ball."

"Two-One-One, Ball, Two One," I transmitted letting the ship know we had a visual on the ship and 2100 pounds of fuel, 2600 pounds under our normal 'on the ball' fuel state. We would definitely need a tanker if we failed to trap on this pass.

The deck was pitching badly. The four-acre flight deck built on top of a small World War II carrier hull made the Midway top heavy. Not only did she pitch and roll; the added weight made her yaw as well creating a Dutch roll around the center of the ship. From the back of the ship it looked like the fantail was drawing a figure eight. On top of that, the ship had to plow into the sea swells to get the wind to blow directly down the angled recovery deck. As the ship reached the top of each wave the bow suddenly pitched forward causing the back of the boat to rise out of the water. This effectively eliminated the twelve-foot hook-to-ramp clearance that we were accustomed to when approaching the ship in calm seas. During the last thirty seconds of our approach, the fantail would periodically be higher than our projected flight path. If our timing was off we would end up hitting the back end of the ship. It was the worst possible landing conditions. It was so bad the Air-Wing Commander put his most experienced LSO, Lieutenant Commander 'Hot Dog' Brown on the LSO platform to talk us down.

At that precise moment the ship's propellers were almost out of the water. "Roger ball, keep it coming, the deck's coming back down" the Landing Signal Officer assured us that we would soon be able to see the landing area and arresting gear. He could not guarantee exactly, however, where it would be when we arrived at the ship.

Steve made a great approach. He flew a centered ball all the way. But as fate would have it the bow of the ship plunged into a mammoth wave. In a few moments the stern would rise even higher out of the water than before.

88

"Power," the LSO shouted envisioning our aircraft crashing into the ship's fantail. "POWER, but don't climb!" the LSO screamed telling us to speed up before the propellers rose completely out of the water.

Steve added a handful of throttle. The aircraft responded immediately wanting to go faster. The faster airspeed made the plane want to climb. So Steve countered by pushing the stick forward causing the aircraft's nose high attitude to flatten out.

We made it over the ramp with a few feet to spare. Slamming down on the deck Steve shoved the throttles to full power in case we missed the wires. Our arresting hook skipped over the second and third wires. Our flat attitude caused us to miss our target wire and the very last two inch arresting cable that could have brought our aircraft to a stop.

"BOLTER! BOLTER! BOLTER!" cried the LSO confirming that we had missed the wires.

Steve immediately rotated the aircraft and we quickly sprang back into the air.

"Switch Two-One-One, rendezvous with Arab Five-Two-Two for tanking, angels twelve", the CCA controller said directing us to the ship's overhead tanker at 12,000 feet.

We were now down to 1500 pounds of fuel. Steve started the climb up to 12,000 feet as I requested the tanker's position.

"Five-Two-Two, say posit," I asked.

"Five-Two-Two's at angels twelve, two-zero-zero radial at four miles," the A-6 tanker's Bombardier/Navigator told us.

He was right in front of us, howbeit a couple of miles up. So Steve put in some left stick as we climbed in order to rendezvous with the tanker on the opposite side of the standard counter-clockwise orbit. Then we went back into the goo. At 12,000 feet we popped out of the clouds into a relatively clear area. But what we saw dumbfounded us. The tanker was heading right for us. For some reason he was in a clockwise tanking pattern. We passed head-on. Steve yanked our aircraft into a hard left turn. The tanker continued its clockwise pattern. We finally joined up on them on the opposite side of the circle. We were now down to 1000 pounds of fuel.

"Five-Two-Two, Two-One-One, Give me a left hand orbit and head back to the ship," Steve ordered so we would be heading the right direction when we came off the tanker. He also wanted to insure that we were overhead the ship in case we ran out of fuel and had to eject.

We approached the tanker preparing to plug our refueling probe into the tanker's basket. After more than one hundred and twenty combat missions together it was easy for me to talk Steve into the two-foot diameter basket. Then we waited for the tanker's green transfer light to illuminate letting us know he was transferring fuel to us.

"We've still got a yellow light Five-Two-Two," I transmitted.

"How about now?" the Bombardier/Navigator asked after recycling his switches.

"Negative," I replied looking at 800 pounds on our fuel gauge. We had four minutes of fuel left.

Steve came up on the intercom and said that if we did not get some fuel soon we would have to eject. I lowered my ejection seat and started stowing my gear. What we did not know at the time was that the Air-Boss was preparing to launch search-and-rescue aircraft and additional helicopters in case we didn't make it.

"Two-One-One, Back out. I'm going to reel in the hose and try it again," the tanker pilot said.

So Steve backed out of the refueling basket. The hose and basket slowly withdrew into the tanker. After what seemed like an eternity the basket finally reappeared and slipped into the wind-stream. Our fuel was now down to 600 pounds. I heard Steve lower his ejection seat.

"Two-One-One, Try it now," the tanker pilot ordered.

Without hesitation we moved toward the basket. You could almost feel the ship's crew and air-wing listening, waiting, knuckles white with tension, praying that we would get the fuel we so desperately needed to make it back aboard the ship. And we knew the pressure was on. Could Steve and I pull it off? Would I be able to talk him into the basket again? Would he hear the subtle inflections in my voice when I gave him up, down, left, right direction into the basket?

No! In the anxiety of the moment we missed the basket. 500 pounds.

"Okay, Steve, we'll make it this time," I said as calmly as I could.

"We've got to," was Steve's only reply as he concentrated on lining up behind the tanker.

"Up... Right.. Right.. Down.. a little Left. Got it!" I exclaimed as the probe entered the basket.

But everyone was still holding their breath. Would the fuel transfer system start pumping its precious cargo? The light stayed yellow.

"Push the basket in a couple of feet," the tanker pilot ordered hoping that would clear up the problem.

Steve gave the aircraft a little power. The basket moved forward. 400 pounds. The light stayed yellow. Steve gave it more power. The basket retracted even further. The light stayed yellow. 300 pounds.

"We're not getting any fuel transfer," Steve said anxiously aware that we would be out of fuel in ninety seconds.

Steve told me to prepare for ejection. Prickly fingers ran up my spine as I pushed myself back into the seat and assumed the correct posture for ejection. My mind quickly filled with bits and pieces of ejection procedures and water survival training that had been drilled into me over the years. But my heart really wasn't in it. No one ever wanted to leave a nice warm cockpit and be blasted out into a cold, black, cloud covered night in the middle of the ocean.

"Schoolboy, We're going to back out and prepare to eject," Steve transmitted.

"Try one more push Two-One-One," the tanker pilot pleaded immediately.

Steve added a handful of power. The hose whipped-lashed from the force. We were now directly under the A-6's tail. We were so close I could have reached up and grabbed the tanker's tail-hook. We could not push the hose in any further. 200 pounds.

Then Steve and I saw one of the most beautiful sights we had ever seen. A green light under the tanker's wing finally illuminated and we started taking on fuel. Talk about a feeling of joy and elation. We didn't have to eject after all. We could almost hear the hundreds of officers and sailors who had been monitoring our progress and preparing to rescue us breathe a huge sigh of relief. They knew that we had come within a hair's breadth of losing a twelve million-dollar aircraft. They also knew that our chances of being rescued from the ocean at night in the middle of a typhoon were next to nothing.

Our fuel gauge started ticking up the pounds. 500, 750, 1000, 1250, 1500 pounds of fuel. Then the green light went out. After all that, we had 600 pounds less fuel than when we attempted to land ten minutes earlier.

"Sorry Two-One-One, that's all the gas we've got," the tanker pilot apologized.

Steve backed out of the basket. Schoolboy was immediately on the radio giving us our landing instructions. They were waiting on us. And we were the only two planes left to recover. If we did not land this time there was no more fuel available, anywhere.

We lined up behind the ship and began our approach. The boat was still pitching badly. The optical landing system, which was usually stabilized on its own platform, was now pitching beyond its gimbal limits. Without a stable platform, the landing would be even more difficult since we could not be sure where we were on the glide-slope.

Once again CCA transmitted "Switch Two-One-One, three-quarters of a mile, call the ball."

"Two-One-One, Ball, One Zero," I called with 1000 pounds of fuel left.

"Roger, Ball, Good start. Don't chase the ball, it's moving on you," the LSO told us.

The LSO was right. The ball was showing us on glide-slope one moment, then a low ball the next. It was all over the place because the ship was pitching so badly. Steve just had to keep what he had going and let the LSO make the calls to get us down.

"Keep it coming, the deck will be down by the time you get here," the LSO assured us.

94

The ship's stern was out of the water, its gigantic propellers grasping at air while trying to propel the 70,000-ton ship through the water. All we could see were faint red lights on the ship's mast and half a dozen vertical drop-lights pointing toward the centerline of the flight deck. The landing area itself and the arresting gear were hidden from our view.

We were less than a quarter of a mile from the ship on our final attempt at landing when the ship's bow began to rise. The arresting gear and landing area reappeared.

Steve maintained his wits and fought the urge to dive for the deck. It was one of the worse mistakes a Naval Aviator could ever make around the ship. It almost always ended in disaster, at the least a missed wire and another attempt at landing. We crossed the ramp with maybe five feet of room between our plane and the ship. An instant later our arresting hook caught the number one wire. The next instant we were thrown forward, our shoulder straps thankfully preventing us from plunging into the instrument panel. We were home.

Steve taxied out of the landing area just as our A-6 tanker called the ball. Because the A-6 had a much slower approach speed than our F-4, it was able to snag the number two wire and bring to a close a gut wrenching hour of slow motion madness that every Naval Aviator who has ever flown from a carrier has experienced.

And I never referred to a Barrier Patrol as boring again.

Run Away Stabilator

An F-4 is proof that even a brick can fly if you put a big enough engine on it;

and the F-4 took two!

Have you ever wondered what it would be like to know you are about to die? Or try to imagine what goes through a person's mind as they contemplate death? I have! And it's not at all what you probably think.

After five years and two combat cruises to the Gulf of Tokin, Vietnam, I settled into civilian life but still flew F-4's on the weekends as a Naval Reservist. Every other weekend found me in the cockpit of a supersonic jet fighter.

This particular 'Weekend Warrior' sortie began with a flight briefing, weather report, and a two-plane launch from Dallas Naval Air Station in Grand Prairie, Texas. As we

completed the last planned intercept on our training exercise somewhere over the dusty plains north of College Station, Texas, our two plane sortie engaged in what fighter pilots the world over craved: a dogfight.

Up, up we flew chasing our bogey as he rocketed towards the sun in an attempt to evade our pursuit. Reaching the top of our vertical loop we rolled the fighter over on her back and pulled the nose down past the horizon. Coming down the other side, still inverted, we maneuvered hard to put the F-4's gunsight on the bogey's tail pipe.

At sixty degrees nose down, head in the cockpit, I locked the bogey up on radar. Matching the bogey's evasive maneuvers my pilot pulled hard to put the bogey in the 'pipper'. Just as we were preparing to squeeze off a simulated Sidewinder heat-seeking missile shot on the bogey's hot exhaust, our plane lurched nose down, pinning our helmets against the canopy. The negative G's sent blood rushing to our heads causing a momentary red-out. Within seconds we were pushed back into the hard ejection seats. Straining against the alternating forces of positive and negative gravity, we went through the emergency procedures for an out of control aircraft. We turned off every piece of equipment we could in hopes of stopping the stabilator from flailing us all over the cockpit.

So there we were, banging our heads against the canopy, back up into the seat, down against the canopy, back up into the seat, just as fast as the run-away stabilator would go. Full nose up, full nose down, full nose up, every four seconds.

Speeding toward earth at 500 miles per hour we were able to roll the aircraft upright. But we could not pull out of the dive. We were out of control and the emergency procedures that had been drilled into us told us that we would soon have to leave the aircraft. Passing 10,000 feet my pilot yelled "Eject, Eject, Eject!" I yelled back "Negit, Negit, Negit! We'll break our backs". He knew I was right. There was no way to stay in the ejection seat long enough to get in the proper position for ejection. Moreover, pulling the ejection handle would ignite a rocket engine under our seats that would unleash a blast 24 times the force of gravity; the seat would break anything in its path including our backs, legs and arms.

At that moment we knew it was our time to "buy the farm". There were no more emergency procedures to perform, there was no way out, only down. In the few moments we had left we talked about what a great life it had been. Wishing each other well, we both became quite and waited for the inevitable.

I remember gazing at the ground looming up in the canopy and uttering the most remarkable statement I had ever heard. I told myself that I was "too young to die this old".

As I let out a breath of air, I suddenly realized that I could hear not only my exhaling breath, but my pilot's heavy breathing as well. We still had electrical power on the plane! So I yelled, "turn off the generators". It was this last ditch effort that caused us to flame out at 4,000 feet, which would have been inconsequential had we crashed.

But that's all it took. Without electrical power my pilot regained control of the stabilator and pulled the aircraft out of its steep dive. I still remember seeing the trees rushing by, so close I could almost touch them.

But we were not out of the woods yet. The pilot yelled back, "flip a coin". He was asking me which engine to start. And it was a gamble. If we started the wrong engine, we would be back in the same predicament we just left. I hollered back, "Stay with procedures and re-start the starboard engine." Slowly the right engine came to life and we began climbing for some altitude. Not wishing to press our luck, we limped back to base with only the single right engine keeping us airborne.

Arriving back at Naval Air Station Dallas we shut down the engine and made our way back to the stabilator hoping to find some telltale evidence that would explain what had happened. Only after an aircraft Trouble Shooter opened an access panel did we discover what caused our emergency. A bundle of wires running down the left side of the aircraft that supplies electrical current to the stabilator motor was chaffed, exposing bare wires to the airframe. In essence, we almost died because of a short circuit.

After nine years of flying supersonic jet fighters I decided that longevity was probably more important to me than living a life where every other weekend was, as the Navy use to say, "an Adventure."

I've never regretted that decision to leave aviation. And I will always remember my last great adventure.

Welcome Home

Officially the Vietnam War ended over twenty-five years ago. But for anyone who fought there the war still rages on, not with guns and bullets, but with memories that are either too horrible or too exhilarating to forget. But the worse part about the war was coming home to an America that despised us for fighting for our country.

Whether you were a soldier, seaman, officer or aviator, you still had to face hostile forces when you returned. There were no parades, no parties, and no newspaper articles about you returning safely from Vietnam. Instead, people would question why you were so stupid to go to Vietnam in the first place. Why didn't you avoid the draft? Why didn't you plea conscientious objector? Why didn't you go to Canada? For the vast majority of those who went to Vietnam the answer was the same: We did it because we had no other choice and copping out was not an option.

I was one of the fortunate ones who had more than my fair share of excitement and only a few nightmares. I can't imagine the horror of those soldiers who spent the entire war wading through rice paddies and hacking their way through tropical jungles. Their losses were far greater than I can even fathom.

Oh, sure, the Vietnam Memorial brought some closure. Just as Desert Storm seemed to raise the status of all Vietnam vets from a snake in the grass to something just above an automaton that carried out orders without emotions.

But emotions are all we have left of the war. We feel them all the time. We silently weep when we think about a friend or buddy whose life was taken for some senseless Domino Theory. We long for some recognition of our sacrifices, an appreciation of the horrors we saw, a meaningful apology from someone, somewhere that says they were wrong to force us to give up our innocence and die on someone else's soil.

There came a point in everyone's tour of duty when the irony of the war was brought down to a single finite moment. In that instant you realized that you were nothing but a pawn in a gigantic chess game that had nothing to do with patriotism. That moment came for me after two of my squadron-mates had been shot down and captured by the North Vietnamese. That night I sat on my bunk and wept. I was mad; mad at the Vietnamese for shooting down my friends; mad at President Johnson for escalating the war in the first place; mad at the idiots in Washington who sustained the war for their own personal gain. I pictured a chessboard with live soldiers and aviators dressed as pawns. "Move here, pawn! Move there, pawn! Oh you were captured? So sorry. Bring me another pawn. Oops, lost another aviator. Bring me more pawns!"

It was almost ten years after Vietnam that someone expressed his appreciation for my involvement in that unpopular war. A coworker asked me if I had been in Vietnam. When I hung my head and acknowledged his question he said "Thank you for going." Years later while writing these stories a young receptionist told me someone thanked her father for serving in Vietnam. I broke down and cried, slapping a hand across my face to hide my embarrassment at being on such a short emotional string.

A friend of mine suggested that maybe I felt guilty for surviving when so many of my friends and shipmates were killed or captured. In the first nine months of my second cruise to Vietnam, seventeen aviators had either been killed, captured or were missing in action. Fifteen percent of my fellow aviators who flew with me over North Vietnam never returned to the ship. I could have easily been one of them and came close many times. But, no I do not feel guilty. We all knew the risk. Each time we crossed the beach we knew there was a good chance we could be shot down or killed. And we accepted that.

So why is it that after all these years a grown man can be brought to tears at the slightest reference that triggers memories of the war? I wish I knew. I thought writing these stories would be therapeutic and let me look under the thin skin covering an emotional wound that never seems to heal. Maybe I will never know why I get so sentimental and teary eyed when I think about the war. What I do know is this: it was hard to come away from that war without some deep,

emotional scars. And those scars will probably stay with us the rest of our lives.

About the Author

As a member of an elite fraternity of carrier based Naval Aviators, Art Long lived to tell about flying combat missions over North Vietnam; the most heavily defended area in the entire world. As a Radar Intercept Officer in the McDonald Douglas F-4 Phantom II jet fighter, he flew over 150 combat missions in North and South Vietnam with Fighter Squadron VF-151 aboard the USS Midway from June 1971 to March 1973. He made over 200 carrier arrested landing. Those who flew with him knew him as 'Kim'.

After Vietnam, he became a Weekend Warrior flying F-4's twice a month with VF-201 out of Naval Air Station Dallas from 1974 until 1978. He left the service with the rank of Lieutenant Commander.

Printed in the United States
140081LV00005B/20/A